Gospel Light's

BIG BOOK
OF GOD'S
AMAZING
CREATION

Science and Nature Activities
for Ages 3 to 12

- 75 interactive activities for ages 3 to 5
- 75 interactive activities for ages 6 to 12
- Activities arranged thematically by the
  days of creation
- Prayer and praise suggestions
- "Why It Works" features

Reproducible!

HOW TO MAKE CLEAN COPIES FROM THIS BOOK

you may make copies of portions of this book with a clean conscience if

- you (or someone in your organization) are the original purchaser;

- you are using the copies you make for a noncommercial purpose (such as teaching or promoting your ministry) within your church or organization;

- you follow the instructions provided in this book.

However, it is ILLEGAL for you to make copies if

- you are using the material to promote, advertise or sell a product or service other than for ministry fund-raising;

- you are using the material in or on a product for sale; or

- you or your organization are not the original purchaser of this book.

By following these guidelines you help us keep our products affordable.
Thank you,
Gospel Light

Editorial Staff

Senior Managing Editor, Sheryl Haystead • **Senior Editor,** Debbie Barber • **Editorial Team,** Amanda Abbas, Mary Davis • **Contributing Editors,** Suzanne Bass, Kurt Goble, Jim Hawley, Heather Kempton, Rich Smith • **Art Directors,** Lenndy McCullough, Christina Renée Sharp, Samantha A. Hsu • **Designer,** Zelle Olson

Founder, Dr. Henrietta Mears • **Publisher,** William T. Greig • **Senior Consulting Publisher,** Dr. Elmer L. Towns • **Senior Consulting Editor,** Wesley Haystead, M.S.Ed. • **Senior Editor, Biblical and Theological Issues,** Bayard Taylor, M.Div.

How to Use This Book

if you are the children's pastor,

1. Read "Schedule Options" on pages 10-11 to get an understanding of ways to use *The Big Book of God's Amazing Creation*.

2. If *The Big Book of God's Amazing Creation* will be used as the ongoing feature of a program based on this book, you may want to recruit a coordinator several months before the program begins. Provide the coordinator with this book and plan regular check-ins with him or her. Be available for practical support and encouragement.

3. If teachers will use these activities to supplement an existing curriculum, provide them with copies of the appropriate age-level activities.

if you are the coordinator,

1. Read "Schedule Options" on pages 10-11 to get an understanding of ways to use *The Big Book of God's Amazing Creation*.

2. In conjunction with the children's pastor, recruit the appropriate number of teachers needed. (One adult for every four to eight children is recommended.)

3. Use a calendar to assign the activities to teachers. (Note: These activities stand alone; they may be used in any order.)

4. Prepare ahead of time the materials needed for each activity. (You may wish to recruit a supply coordinator to collect and distribute materials.)

if you are a teacher or small-group leader,

1. Read "Schedule Options" on pages 10-11 to get an understanding of ways to use *The Big Book of God's Amazing Creation*.

2. Read the following articles: "Leading a Child to Christ," "Science at Church?" "Asking Good Questions" and "Science Safety: Helpful Hints" on pages 8, 12, 13 and 19.

3. Prepare and lead activities to supplement your existing curriculum, or as assigned by program coordinator.

Contents

Elementary Experiments

DAY 7: Rest and Inertia

Early Childhood Explorations

Elementary Experiments

Bonus Recipes

Indexes

The Power of God's Creation

It's been said that 10 of the most controversial words in the English language are, "In the beginning, God created the heavens and the earth" (Genesis 1:1). Certainly, few other statements could have such a profound impact: These words declare a worldview that colors everything we see, feel and think! Choosing any other idea of Earth's origin produces a worldview that tells us we are random accidents with no meaning or purpose beyond our momentary self-satisfaction. But as we recognize that we are God's creatures, we begin to understand the vastness and variety of His work. It fairly shouts to us that, although we are small and finite, our Creator's love, wisdom and power are forever beyond our imagining!

Even though this physical creation we see is beautiful, the spiritual "new creation in Christ Jesus" within us is even more beautiful than anything we can conceive! Beyond that, Jesus tells us He is preparing a place for those who are His (see John 14). Heaven is the full expression of His creativity—our future home is something that exceeds anything we have yet experienced. What joy, hope and genuine meaning that awareness brings! We aren't accidents: We matter; we are loved; we have purpose for being. And our purpose doesn't stop when we leave these bodies behind; rather, it begins!

Let the activities in this book spark your imagination. Take them as God's invitation to wide-eyed wonder! Ask God to give you fresh perspective on His good work. Then take this marvelous opportunity to discover and revel in these amazing aspects of God's creation right along with your kids!

The goal of these activities is to encourage you and your kids to joyfully celebrate the wonders we find in the world God made for us! Prepare yourself well for these experiences and activities so that you can focus on interacting with the kids instead of on finding missing materials or completing unfinished details. As you share with them your own understanding of these experiences and activities, point out the beauty, wisdom, love and power of our Creator. As you genuinely express your joy and admiration for what you see in God's creation, your kids will be encouraged to express their wonder and thanks as well!

Leading a Child to Christ

Many adult Christians look back to their childhood years as the time when they accepted Christ as Savior. As children mature, they will grow in their understanding of the difference between right and wrong. They will also develop a sense of their own need for forgiveness and feel a growing desire to have a personal relationship with God.

However, the younger the child is, the more limited he or she will be in understanding abstract terms. Children of all ages are likely to be inconsistent in following through on their intentions and commitments. Therefore, they need thoughtful, patient guidance in coming to know Christ personally and continuing to grow in Him.

Pray

Ask God to prepare the students in your group to receive the good news about Jesus and prepare you to communicate effectively with them.

Present the Good News

Use words and phrases that students understand. Avoid symbolism that will confuse these literal-minded thinkers. Remember that each child's learning will be at different places on the spectrum of understanding. Discuss these points slowly enough to allow time for thinking and comprehending.

a. God wants you to become His child. Do you know why God wants you in His family? (See 1 John 3:1.)

b. You and I and all the people in the world have done wrong things. The Bible word for doing wrong is "sin." What do you think should happen to us when we sin? (See Romans 6:23.)

c. God loves you so much, He sent His Son to die on the cross for your sins. Because Jesus never sinned, He is the only One who can take the punishment for your sins. (See 1 Corinthians 15:3; 1 John 4:14.) On the third day after Jesus died, God brought Him back to life.

d. Are you sorry for your sins? Tell God that you are. Do you believe Jesus died to take the punishment for your sins? If you tell God you are sorry for your sins and tell Him you do believe and accept Jesus' death to take away your sins, God forgives all your sin. (See 1 John 1:9.)

e. The Bible says that when you believe that Jesus is God's Son and that He is alive today, you receive God's gift of eternal life. This gift makes you a child of God. This means God is with you now and forever. (See John 3:16.)

Give students many opportunities to think about what it means to be a Christian; expose them to a variety of lessons and descriptions of the meaning of salvation to aid their understanding.

Talk Personally with the Student

Talking about salvation one-on-one creates the opportunity to ask and answer questions. Ask questions that move the student beyond simple yes or no answers or recitation of memorized information. Ask open-ended, what-do-you-think questions such as:

☼ "Why do you think it's important to . . . ?"

☼ "What are some things you really like about Jesus?"

☼ "Why do you think that Jesus had to die because of wrong things you and I have done?"

☼ "What difference do you think it makes for a person to be forgiven?"

When students use abstract terms or phrases they have learned previously, such as "accepting Christ into my heart," ask them to tell you what the term or phrase means in different words. Answers to these open-ended questions will help you discern how much the student does or does not understand.

Offer Opportunities without Pressure

Children normally desire to please adults. This characteristic makes them vulnerable to being unintentionally manipulated by well-meaning adults. A good way to guard against coercing a student's response is to simply pause periodically and ask, "Would you like to hear more about this now or at another time?" Loving acceptance of the student, even when he or she is not fully interested in pursuing the matter, is crucial in building and maintaining positive attitudes toward becoming part of God's family.

Give Time to Think and Pray

There is great value in encouraging a student to think and pray about what you have said before making a response. Also allow moments for quiet thinking about questions you have asked.

Respect the Student's Response

Whether or not a student declares faith in Jesus Christ, there is a need for adults to accept the student's action. There is also a need to realize that a student's initial responses to Jesus are just the beginning of a lifelong process of growing in faith.

Guide the Student in Further Growth

There are several important parts in the nurturing process.

a. Talk regularly about your relationship with God.

As you talk about your relationship, the student will begin to feel that it's OK to talk about such things. Then you can comfortably ask the student to share his or her thoughts and feelings, and you can encourage the student to ask questions of you.

b. Prepare the student to deal with doubts. Emphasize that certainty about salvation is not dependent on our feelings or doing enough good deeds. Show the student places in God's Word that clearly declare that salvation comes by grace through faith. (See John 1:12; Ephesians 2:8-9; Hebrews 11:6; 1 John 5:11.)

c. Teach the student to confess all sins. This means agreeing with God that we really have sinned. Assure the student that confession always results in forgiveness. (See 1 John 1:9.)

The Preschool Child and Salvation

☼ The young child is easily attracted to Jesus. Jesus is a warm, sympathetic person who obviously likes children, and children readily like Him. These early perceptions prepare the foundation for the child to receive Christ as Savior and to desire to follow His example in godly living. While some preschoolers may indeed pray to become a member of God's family, accepting Jesus as their Savior, expect wide variation in children's readiness for this important step. Allow the Holy Spirit room to work within His own timetable.

☼ Talk simply. Phrases such as "born again" or "Jesus in my heart" are symbolic and far beyond a young child's understanding. Focus on how God makes people a part of His family.

☼ Present the love of Jesus by both your actions and your words in order to lay a foundation for a child to receive Christ as Savior. Look for opportunities in every lesson to talk with a young child who wants to know more about Jesus.

Schedule Options

The explorations and experiments found in this book are intended for integration into a class session, whether by using them as a feature or science center in an existing program or as the basis for an ongoing program.

The explorations and experiments, along with the questions and prayer activities listed, should take from 15 to 30 minutes. (Obviously, more complicated activities will take longer than simple ones.) Many of these activities can be extended both in time and content by using the optional materials and ideas listed in the activities themselves.

These activities work best not with an adult *doing* and children *watching*, but with children doing the activities themselves. It is highly recommended that you provide a small-group format for these activities. This provides children with hands-on interaction and the chance to bond with each other and with one consistent adult leader. Using a small-group format will also make it easier to track attendance and to be aware of children's prayer needs, as well as to create a community in which each child feels known and valued.

Here are instructions for ways to use the activities found in this book:

As a lesson supplement. To supplement lessons during Sunday School, a second-hour session, midweek program, church retreat or other class, make photocopies of the activity page needed in advance. Give one copy to the teacher or small-group leader so that he or she can prepare the activity and gather needed materials.

As a science center. Photocopy the activity page needed. Give one copy to the teacher or small-group leader so that he or she can prepare a science center or "lab table" that could be one center among others during a learning time in which children rotate among centers. This format

allows for information, interaction and relationship to flow and flourish!

As a feature of an ongoing program based on this book. Feature the science and Prayer and Praise ideas in this book in an ongoing program designed not only to inform children about the wonders of God's creation, but also to motivate their gratitude and praise. Add program components such as active games, Bible stories and/or Bible memory verse activities.

For a 60-Minute Session

Science Activity*
20 minutes

Prayer and Praise*
15 minutes

Active Game
15 minutes

Bible Memory Verse Activity
10 minutes

For a 90-Minute Session

Science Activity*
25 minutes

Prayer and Praise*
25 minutes (Add optional activity.)

Active Game
15 minutes

Bible Story
15 minutes

Bible Memory Verse
10 minutes

* found in this book

Customize Sessions for your Group

As you prepare an activity for a session, note the skills needed and the level of understanding required. Then take an extra five minutes to look at your class roster. Think about how best to adapt the activity to your particular group's needs. For instance, if some children in your group do not like to write or are unable to write, use drawing as an option or invite students to dictate responses to small-group leaders. Adapt activities and explorations as needed to fit both your facility and the ages and abilities of your students. This advance planning will ensure that all children can participate successfully.

Carefully planning ways to meet the needs of children sends each child these messages: You are important. We all help each other. We learn better together. We're all part of the same family! It is a powerful way in which adults can model the loving, Christlike attitudes and actions we want our students to learn and show!

If you are using an activity with elementary-aged students, make one copy of the activity for each teacher and helper as well as one copy for every group of four students (the most common grouping in this book) or one for each individual student.

If you are using these activities for preschool-aged children, make one copy of the activity for each teen or adult leader of a group of four to eight children. For a large-group activity, making a copy for each teen or adult leader is helpful but not necessary.

Use the Lab Reports found on pages 15-18 either as a way to extend the experiment time or to increase thinking and discussion about the topic. Keep copies on hand for students to complete whenever there is extra time to fill or distribute them as a way to help your young explorers express more detailed information about their discoveries!

Science at Church?

In our world, kids may more often be seen as people to be amused than involved. Special effects, lifelike graphics and digitized sound have become benchmarks of "virtual quality." Such a value placed on unreality might tempt us to think kids no longer care about exploring the real world. But although our culture advertises its values, products and ideas to children (and parents) all the time, culture has no mandate to teach us what's important—rather, its frankly stated goal is to make sure we buy what is for sale!

But in a high-tech, low-touch, profit-driven world, kids need now more than ever to understand how the real world works. Such understanding used to be absorbed naturally as kids worked on farms or in yards with interested adults who explained God's wonders. The very rarity of this kind of interaction today gives us as Christian educators a great opportunity to be those interested adults who help kids both understand the world around them in a hands-on way and give them a sense of awe that reminds them of the grandeur and power of God seen through His creation.

By involving kids in simple, clear and exciting science activities, we send them a message: that God's Word and science are not at war, nor are they mutually exclusive! The Bible gives us answers to the questions science cannot address about the purpose and meaning of this life that we experience. Wherever the Bible addresses a scientific subject, we find that God's Word, written to people in ancient cultures, is accurate. As we help our kids experience scientific processes by asking good questions and showing our own delight in what God has done, we all are better able to understand bits of God's work and to respond in thankful celebration at the amazing ways God put our universe together!

Our kids (and we) need to recapture the fearless wonder and excitement of discovering God as He has revealed Himself in creation. Involving kids at church in hands-on science activities will fuel their wonder at God's great love, wisdom and power. Besides, it's just plain fun!

Asking Good Questions

In the process of exploring and experimenting, one of the best ways to help children understand what they are experiencing is to ask good questions. There are questions already provided in the individual activities. But the potential for good discussion and greater understanding increases when you become skilled at asking good questions.

characteristics of a Good Question

1. A good question is likely to be open-ended; that is, there is not a yes-or-no or a right-or-wrong answer. Of course, this depends largely on the question, but you will get more discussion out of a question that kids can't answer in one word than one for which only your brightest student will provide the right answer.

2. A good question (especially in science) should be one that will give rise to another question. For instance, instead of asking, "Do you see the steam rising?" you could ask, "What do you see?" or "What do you think is happening?" "Why do you think so?" "What might happen if (we added cold water)?"

the Scientific Method

It is helpful to remember the steps to the scientific method as you think about an activity you will be doing. They are:

1. State the problem. (What happens if . . . ?)

2. Make a hypothesis (an educated guess). (We think it will . . .)

3. Perform the experiment. (What happened? We see that . . .)

4. Record the results. (This is what happened.)

5. Try it again. (Will we get the same results?)

6. State the conclusion. (What did we learn?)

Also involved in any kind of scientific experience is a variety of thinking skills: problem solving, observation, measuring, communicating, predicting and classifying, to name just a few.

On the other hand, science explorations are also likely to give rise not only to questions you are asking but also that are asked of you! If you don't have an answer, the best response is never to bluff or to guess. Simply say, "I don't know the answer to that. Let's each see if we can find an answer this week. We'll talk about it next week." That response models honesty—and good research technique as well!

If you will be expanding these activities into a regular feature of your program or will be basing a program around them, consider decorating an area of the rooms where your sessions will take place. Creating a "science lab" can add fun, excitement and dimension to the proceedings! Here are some ideas for setting the stage to create the perfect atmosphere for fun and learning.

General Science-Related Decorations

Consider drawing a laboratory backdrop or mural, or invite older students to do this as a service project. A mural on one or two walls can make the area (or the whole room) resemble a science lab. On the mural, include drawings of equipment (microscopes, magnifying glasses, computers, beakers, Bunsen burners, etc.), charts (map of Earth, space diagrams, parts of an animal, etc.) and other items to give the room the feel of a science lab. Add appropriate props, such as books, models of animals or the human body, plants, etc.

If possible, include some real scientific reference books or a computer with search capabilities to enrich and expand students' scientific experiences!

If you cannot leave the science center in place from week to week, consider simply pinning murals or posters onto rolling bulletin boards. Add a rolling science table holding books or other materials that can be rolled in during the sessions and then removed. Posters and items can also be attached to a sheet (with staples or duct tape) that can be hung on a wall during each session.

Wear a Uniform

When adults are having fun, it's amazing how much more fun the kids have! Invite the adults involved in sessions to dress in lab coats or white jackets, or even T-shirts with logos or labels that designate them as part of the scientific research team (such as the Cousteau Society or a university research group).

Create a Place

Name and label one or more room doors, especially if you are using more than one room. Places such as Creation Research Center, Glad Scientists' Lab or Dino Dig HQ can give you and your students some intriguing "handles" for thinking about God's creation and the lessons we learn from the world around us.

Use the Lab Reports found on the following four pages (15-18) either as a way to extend the experiment time or to increase thinking and discussion about the topic. Keep copies on hand for students to complete whenever there is extra time to fill or distribute them as a way to help your young explorers express more detailed information about their discoveries!

Name _____   Date _____

Draw or write your answers!

Today I wondered...

Then I predicted...

This is what happened:

LAB REPORT

Name _____

Date _____

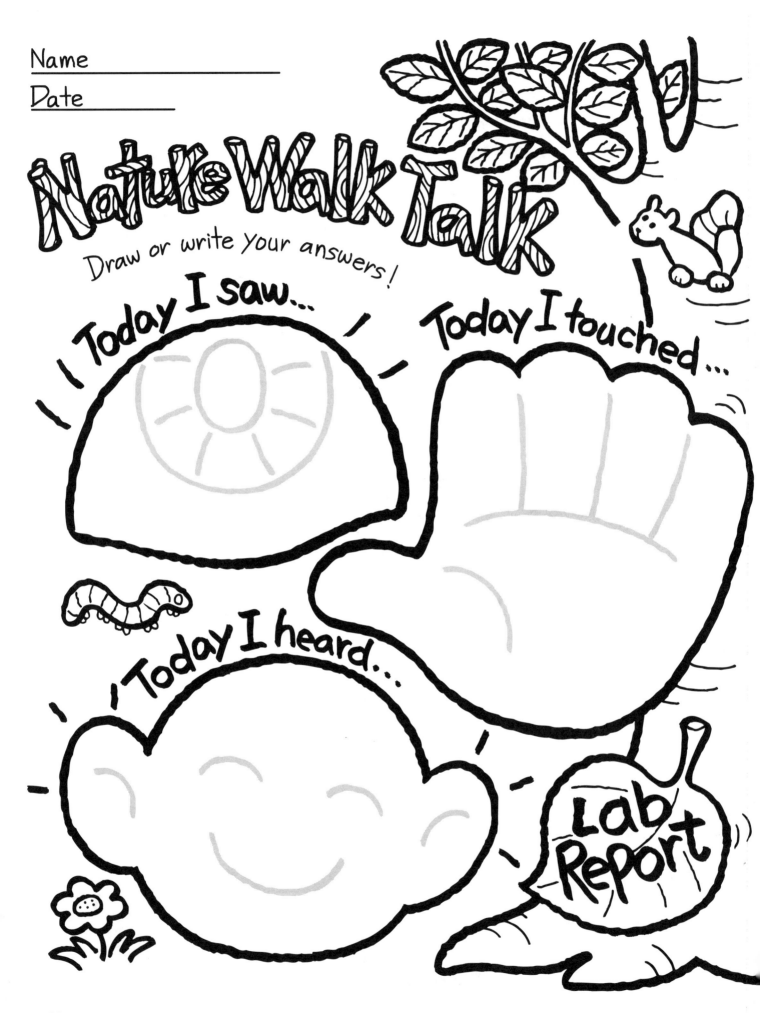

Nature Walk Talk

Draw or write your answers!

Today I saw...

Today I touched...

Today I heard...

Lab Report

Weird Science Story

Name

Date

Draw or write your answers!

We wondered

We expected

We were surprised when

Name _____ Date _____

Draw or write
your answers!

Today I was a
- [ ] rocket scientist
- [ ] ecologist
- [ ] meteorologist
- [ ] archaeologist
- [ ] animal expert
- [ ] creation scientist
- [ ] just myself ☺

My question:

My guess:

My experiment:

My result:

Science Safety: Helpful Hints

Many of us shy away from scientific activities because we can still hear our mothers' voices saying, "You'll put your eye out!" However, not *all* scientific endeavors are the kinds that explode! Have no fear. With proper preparation and a little forethought, scientific activities can be safe, fun and fascinating!

The activities included in this book use ingredients that are generally recognized as safe: They are mainly items found in any household. These are also activities that should be done with at least one adult for every eight children (or with even smaller groups, if possible, to increase the interaction and relationship building).

Eye Protection

Protective goggles will be needed for a few of these activities. They are inexpensive and can be kept as part of the "lab storage." Consider asking a retailer to donate these to your program (most retailers have a donation amount they are allowed to spend yearly).

Gloves

Protective gloves will be needed for only a few of these activities. It might also be a good idea to keep latex gloves or plastic disposable food-service gloves on hand for those children in your class who are likely to be sensitive to substances they might touch with their fingers.

Safety Rules

Post these safety rules (and read them aloud to younger children) so that everyone knows how to use the materials safely and enjoyably.

1. We use the materials only for what we plan, unless we ask an adult first.

2. We wear safety glasses if there is any chance we could hurt our eyes.

3. We wear gloves if there is any chance we could hurt our fingers or that the materials might make our hands itchy.

4. We help each other and take turns.

Remember that an alert adult is the best protection against injury. Plan to recruit volunteer lab assistants (small-group leaders) as well as people who are willing to act as lead scientists (people who rotate among the small groups to help groups stay on track and also to ask engaging questions).

DAY ONE

Light and Dark

"And God said, 'Let there be light,' and there was light. God saw that the light was good, and he separated the light from the darkness. God called the light 'day,' and the darkness he called 'night.' And there was evening, and there was morning—the first day."

Genesis 1:3-5

Here are explorations and experiments to help your kids understand the nature of light—God's first creation!

Light Show

For every child, gather

- Flashlight, lit end covered in colored cellophane secured with a rubber band

- Optional—CDs of various styles of music and CD player

introduce

When do we use a flashlight? Children answer. Today we are going to shine our flashlights to show different colors of light. See if you and a friend can shine your lights together to make a new color.

Do

1. Darken the room.

2. Invite children to shine flashlights on the walls and ceiling.

3. Optional: Play the CD. Change music styles from time to time (encourage children to make the lights dance differently to different styles of music).

4. Invite children to try shining a light onto another person's light. **What happens? Does it happen the same way every time?**

why it works

The light takes away the darkness. But it does something else, too. When we shine our lights onto each other's lights, sometimes the light colors make a third color of light!

Prayer and Praise

Name something God made that is the same color as your light. Children respond. **God made all those colors! Let's each thank God for a color.** Children take turns to say, "Thank You, God, for (color of child's light)" as children briefly shine flashlights. (Optional: Children draw pictures of items whose colors match their light colors and show pictures as they repeat prayer.)

DAY ONE: Light and Dark

Hot Sun

For every four children, gather

- Broken crayons, small items (toys, paper clips, etc.)
- Muffin tin (dark metal or bright aluminum)
- Optional—ice cubes

Introduce

God made the sun to give us light. On a sunny day like this, we can also feel that the sun makes heat. Let's predict which items we think will melt in the heat of the sun.

Do

1. Have children choose an item to place in each cup of the muffin tin. (Optional: Set ice cubes in some of the muffin cups.)

2. Leave the muffin tin in bright sun for 10 minutes. While you wait, have children draw pictures of what they think they will see when they check their muffin tins.

3. Check your muffin tins. Did the results match your picture? What is melting? What is not melting at all? What has already melted?

Why it works

The sun is very hot. It has a lot of energy. The sun's energy is even used by machines to make electricity. Those machines turn sun power to electric power!

Prayer and Praise

What do you like to do outdoors on a sunny day? Children respond. **Let's thank God for things we can do on sunny days.** Children each take a turn to say, "Thank You, God, for (activity child enjoys)." (Optional: Children pantomime favorite actions as they repeat the prayer after you, phrase by phrase.)

DAY ONE: Light and Dark

Shadow Scenes

For a large group, gather

- Light-colored bed sheet
- Desk lamp or strong flashlight
- Familiar objects able to stand (teddy bear, book, cup, tower of blocks, etc.)
- Grocery bag

Introduce

The first thing God created was light. Light causes shadows. Let's see if we can tell by their shadows what things we place behind our sheet.

Do

1. Invite two volunteers to hold up ends of bed sheet. (Rotate volunteers from time to time.)

2. Place light behind sheet.

3. Other children remain in front of sheet and name objects as you place them in a grocery bag.

4. Darken the room. Set one object behind sheet and shine light past the object to create a clear shadow on the sheet. Children guess which object from bag made the shadow. Repeat with other objects.

5. Optional: Set objects that were not in the bag behind the sheet to see if children can identify them.

why it works

Light shines in a straight line. So when it shines on the (teddy bear), only the front of the bear is in the light. Behind the (teddy bear) where there is no light is what we call a shadow.

Prayer and Praise

When are some times we turn on a light? Children respond. **Let's thank God for light.** Pray, inviting children to repeat things they know about light whenever you pause before the word "light" in your prayer. (Optional: Children take turns to stand behind sheet, repeating a sentence prayer while an adult shines the light to make child's shadow.)

DAY ONE: Light and Dark

Stained Glass

For every four children, gather

- Measuring cup
- Warm water in a thermal carafe
- 4 to 6 packets of clear gelatin
- Plastic spoons
- 4 to 6 clear plastic deli containers
- Food coloring in a variety of colors

Introduce

In some buildings, we see windows made of colored glass or stained glass. Where have you seen colored glass windows? Children answer. Let's make some pretend stained glass windows.

Do

1. For each color, measure and pour half the amount of warm water indicated on the gelatin package into a deli container.

2. Child sprinkles the package of clear gelatin over the warm water and stirs until gelatin is dissolved.

3. Child chooses a color of food coloring and squirts a few drops into mixture and stirs.

4. Let gelatin set.

5. Hold up the containers to the light to see the "stained glass windows." Can you see the colors better with or without light shining through them? Are the colors light or dark? Can you arrange your "windows" so light shines through them in rainbow order?

Why it works

Light contains every color. In this experiment, the gelatin is like colored glass in a window. The light shines through the "window" and the color shines through on the other side of the window.

Prayer and Praise

How would your (shirt) look if there were no color? Children respond. God made light to contain every color! Let's thank God for making the colors in light. When I stop during my prayer, you may name a color. Dear God, thank You for making (red). (Optional: Children draw pictures of rainbows and dictate prayers to be added.)

DAY ONE: Light and Dark

Light Bender

For every four children, gather

- Clear glass or plastic bowl half full of water

- Beads, pebbles or other small items (use larger items if accidental swallowing is a concern)

Introduce

When light shines on something, we are able to see it. Does light shine the same through water as it does through air? Let's find out!

Do

1. Choose an item or two. Drop items into the water.

2. After water is still, look through the sides of the bowl at the items you dropped. What do you notice?

3. Take turns to put your hand into the bowl. How does your hand look different?

4. While looking only through the side of the bowl, try to pick up an item. What happens? Is it easy or hard to do?

why it works

When light shines through water, the water bends the light. When the light is bent, it fools our eyes. It is harder to see exactly where the item is we are trying to pick up!

Prayer and Praise

What are some things you do that you cannot do when it is dark? Children respond. Choose one of those activities and let's all thank God for the light so that we can do those things. Thank You, God, for light so we can . . . (each child takes a turn to tell activity he or she chose). In Jesus' name, amen. (Optional: Children draw pictures of activities on large butcher paper. Add a written prayer and read it aloud to the children.)

DAY ONE: Light and Dark

Shadow Stretch

For every four children, gather

- 7-foot (2.1-m) length of butcher paper laid on floor
- Desk lamp
- 4 colored markers (one color for each child)

Introduce

What makes a shadow big? What makes the shadow of something big look small? Let's try this experiment to find out.

Do

1. Set the lamp near one end of paper and then darken the room.

2. Children take turns to stand at one end of the paper. Outline and label each child's shadow on the paper.

3. Vary the position of the lamp to create longer or shorter shadows.

4. Older children may enjoy lying on the traced shadows to compare their body sizes to the sizes of their shadows.

Why it works

When we move the lamp, the light shines on our bodies in a different way. This makes our shadows change in shape and size.

Prayer and Praise

When we go outside today, do you think your shadow will be long or short? Children respond. Let's thank God for times when our shadows are long and short. Children join you in slowly saying the word "long" and then quickly saying the word "short" as you use those words in prayer. (Optional: Children go outside to observe their shadows. Pray aloud outdoors.)

DAY ONE: Light and Dark

Ultraviolet Light

For every four children, gather

- 2 clear plastic cups
- Tonic water
- Tap water
- Sheet of black construction paper

Introduce

God made some kinds of light that we cannot see with our eyes. Let's try this experiment to see ultraviolet light, a kind of light we can't usually see.

Do

1. Set cups in a sunny place.

2. Children watch as you fill one cup with tonic water and the other with tap water.

3. One child holds the piece of black paper behind the cups.

4. Other children look through the sides of the glasses at the top surfaces of both kinds of water. **What do you see? Which water surface looks blue? We know the water is clear. What do you think makes it blue?**

5. Children trade assignments so everyone has a turn to look.

Why it works

The tonic water has a chemical in it called quinine. When the sunlight shines on the tonic water, the quinine makes the ultraviolet part of the sunlight show.

Prayer and Praise

Let's pray together. When I say, "Thank You, God," let's each take a turn to name something that gives light. Conclude, **We are glad for the ways You made light for us! In Jesus' name, amen.** (Optional: Children draw pictures of sources of light and then name pictured items in prayer.)

DAY ONE: Light and Dark

Sunlight Shapes

introduce

God made the sun to give us light. Today we will see how sunlight can make surprising shapes on our papers.

Do

1. Children lay construction paper in direct sunlight. **Choose items to place on your paper.**

2. Several hours later, children check to see if the sun has bleached color from papers to create unbleached areas ("shadows") in the shapes of the items. (The longer items remain in the sun, the more distinct their outlines.)

3. Later, children gather sheets and items. **Can you match the items with their sunlight shapes?**

4. Optional: Children set items on paper, turn on a desk lamp and leave the paper for the same length of time as they leave the other papers outdoors. Children compare this sheet with sheets left in sunlight.

why it works

Sunlight is very powerful! It bleached the color out of the papers as they lay in the sun. But where the objects were, the color is not changed.

Prayer and Praise

What other things does sunlight do? (Grows plants. Keeps us warm. Gives us sunburn.) **God made the sun just right so that Earth isn't too cold or too hot to live on.** Invite children to create motions for this prayer: **Thank You, God, for sun so bright. It makes us warm and gives us light. Sunlight helps to grow our food. Thank You, God. The sun is good.**

DAY ONE: Light and Dark

Hidden Pictures

For every eight children, gather

• Daytime or nighttime scene poster or magazine picture, covered with large sticky notes

introduce

There is a daytime or nighttime picture under these sticky notes. When you think you can tell what the picture is, pat yourself on the head!

Do

1. Children take turns to remove sticky notes. When a note is removed from the sky area, ask, "Is this a daytime picture or a nighttime picture?" Invite children to tell what is happening in the picture and whether or not it could happen in both daytime and at nighttime.

2. Groups trade pictures and repeat the game.

why it works

Is the sky in the picture light or dark? The light in the sky makes it easy to tell whether it is daytime or nighttime.

Prayer and Praise

What else tells us whether it is daytime or nighttime? (Sun. Moon. Stars.) The first thing God made was day and night. God gave us nighttime so that we could rest. He gave us daytime so that we could play and learn. Let's thank God for daytime (run in place) and nighttime (pretend to sleep). Children act out time of day as you use the words in prayer. (Optional: Children tear or cut out pictures of day- and nighttime activities from magazines to add to a group collage. Write a prayer on the collage; read it aloud.)

DAY ONE: Light and Dark

Color Prism

ather

- 6 empty plastic water bottles with lids
- Water
- 6 colors of food coloring
- Masking tape

Introduce

What is your favorite color? The colors in light are called a rainbow. Today we will use colors to make a rainbow!

Do

1. **Fill bottles with water.**

2. **Drop some food coloring into each bottle** (red, orange, yellow, green, blue and purple).

3. An adult securely fastens lids to bottles, wrapping masking tape around each lid.

4. **Take turns shaking bottles to mix water and food coloring.**

5. Children take bottles to a sunny location (outdoors, window, etc.). **Set the bottles in a row to observe what happens when the sun shines through them. Name the colors you see!** Try to put your colors in rainbow order.

Why it works

Light has many colors in it. When we see a rainbow, it shows the colors that are in the light. The water in the sky bends the light as it shines through the water so that the colors show!

Prayer and Praise

When have you seen a rainbow? (Rainstorms. Water hose. Sprinkler.) **Choose one color of water bottle. As we say, "Thank You, God, for colors," lift your water bottle high!** (Optional: Children use colored water and paintbrushes to paint designs on concrete. Thank God aloud for colors children are using.)

32

© 2006 Gospel Light: Permission to photocopy granted. *The Big Book of God's Amazing Creation*

DAY ONE: Light and Dark

Light Bounce

For every four children, gather

- Sheet of paper and tape
- 2 to 4 mirrors
- Flashlight

introduce

The first thing God created was light. Do you think light travels in a straight line or do you think it curves? Let's try this experiment to see.

Do

1. Tape the sheet of paper anywhere you want on the wall. This is your target.

2. While one person holds the flashlight, the others hold mirrors.

3. Darken the room. Shine the flashlight away from the target toward one of the mirrors.

4. Use that mirror to reflect the light to another mirror. Then try to reflect the light at the target. Work on adjusting the angles of the mirrors to make this happen. Then trade assignments, add another mirror or have a team member hold and move the target!

why it works

Light waves tend to travel in a straight line. Because this is so, we can reflect the light with mirrors to move the light to the target, even though the source of light, the flashlight, is pointed away from the target!

Prayer and Praise

What are some other things you know about light? Students respond. **Let's thank God for light, adding as many descriptive words as we can.** Pray, **Thank You, God, for light. Thank You that light is . . .** Students take turns to add descriptive words. (Optional: Students make wax-resist pictures of their experiments: Draw in crayon; paint over with dark blue or black watercolor; add a written prayer.)

DAY ONE: Light and Dark

water Magnifier

For every child, gather

- Oatmeal container or 8-inch (20.5-cm) long section of 4-inch (10-cm) diameter PVC pipe, with at least one side cutout
- Decoration materials (pens, markers, etc.)
- Plastic wrap
- Scissors
- Strong rubber band
- Water in a pitcher
- Items to view (rocks, seeds, etc.)

introduce

What do you think happens when we shine light into water? Students respond. **Today we are going to discover how water can make light bend!**

Do

1. Decorate your cylinder in any way you like.

2. Cut a piece of plastic wrap large enough to loosely fit over the end of the cylinder. Let the wrap droop in the middle to form a well.

3. Secure the plastic wrap over the end with the rubber band.

4. Set your cylinder in a well-lighted area. Pour a little water into the plastic-wrap well.

5. Set an object in the bottom of your cylinder. Look at it through the water. **How does it look different?**

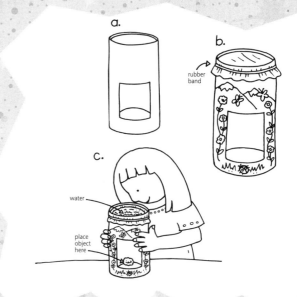

a.

b.
rubber band

c.
water
place object here

why it works

The plastic wrap shapes the water into the same shape as a magnifying glass. It is called a convex lens. A convex lens bends rays of light in such a way that it makes the object look bigger!

Prayer and Praise

What are some places you have seen convex lenses? (Microscopes. Binoculars. Telescopes.) **The first person to think about convex lenses probably noticed how a drop of water made something beneath it look larger. God gave us minds to discover new things all the time!** Invite three volunteers to thank God for light, for water and for our eyes.

DAY ONE: Light and Dark

Kaleidoscope

For every child, gather

- 3 wallet-sized rectangular plastic mirrors (all same size; available at craft stores)
- Colored electrical tape
- Plain index card
- Pencil
- Scissors
- Items to view (confetti, beads, torn paper, etc.)

introduce

Light travels in a straight line. That means we see a pretty accurate reflection from a flat mirror. But what happens when you mirror a mirror's reflection? Try this amazing way to use light.

Do

1. Set your mirrors in a triangle with the reflective sides facing each other.

2. Tape them together securely on the outsides of the mirrors.

3. Set your triangle with an open end on the index card and trace around it.

4. Cut out the triangle and tape it to the bottom of your mirrors.

5. Now you have a kaleidoscope. Set objects into the center to view them. **How do they look? Shake the kaleidoscope. What changes? Why?**

why it works

Because light travels in a straight line, the reflection of the items in your kaleidoscope bounces from mirror to mirror. This creates a repeating set of patterns.

Prayer and Praise

What do you like best about your kaleidoscopes? Students tell. Invite students to tell amazing things they have seen that involve light, such as fireworks, the Milky Way, the Northern Lights or laser shows. **God created light to do many amazing and beautiful things!** Invite three volunteers to thank God for something beautiful he or she has seen. (Optional: Students draw pictures of beautiful things they have seen, adding written prayers.)

DAY ONE: Light and Dark

Shadow Puppets

For every four children, gather

- 10 to 15 drinking straws
- Masking tape
- Construction paper
- Scissors
- Flashlight

introduce

What can we see where there is no light? Let's experiment with light and shadows to help us discover what we can see where there is no light.

Do

1. Cut construction paper into any shape desired or tape several shapes together.

2. Tape a straw onto your completed shape to make a shadow puppet.

3. Darken the room and shine the flashlight at the wall. **What do you see when you hold the puppets between the light and the wall?**

4. Try moving the flashlight or the puppets. **What makes the shapes larger? Smaller? Clearer?**

5. Twist the straws to spin the puppets. **How do their shadows change?**

why it works

When we move the flashlight, what do you notice about the puppets' shadows? (They can change in shape and size.) **This is like what happens when Earth rotates every day. The planet rotates, so the angle of the sun's light changes all the time. That causes shadows to change in shape and size.**

Prayer and Praise

At what time of day are shadows longer? (Early and late in the day.) **Shorter?** (Nearer to noon.) **No shadows at all?** (Noon.) **God made our world in amazing ways!** Darken room. Students take turns to pass and turn on a flashlight while saying a sentence prayer to thank God for light.

DAY ONE: Light and Dark

indoor Rainbow

For every four children, gather

- Wide-mouthed glass jar, filled halfway with water
- Pocket mirror (small enough to fit inside the jar)
- Flashlight
- Optional—a white bed sheet

introduce

Light seems to be clear or colorless. But there is more to light than what we see right now. Let's try this experiment to find out what is hidden in light!

Do

1. In a room with white walls, set the mirror inside the jar of water. (Optional: Teacher invites volunteers to hold up white sheet.)

2. Set the jar on a table or floor. Tilt the mirror slightly upward.

3. Darken the room and then shine the flashlight at the mirror. A rainbow should appear on the white wall!

4. If no rainbow appears, change the angle of either the light or the mirror.

why it works

When we shine the flashlight at the mirror, the mirror reflects the light back through the water. The water acts as a prism. It bends the beam of light so that each color that is already in the light can be seen.

Prayer and Praise

What colors do you see in the sky? When? (Rainbows. Sunsets. Storms.) **How do these things help you learn about what God is like?** Invite volunteers to finish this prayer: "Thank You, God, for . . ." (Optional: Write the first letter of each color of the rainbow [R, O, Y, G, B, V] down the left side of a large sheet of butcher paper. Students write responses in appropriate colors on the paper.)

DAY ONE: Light and Dark

Personal Periscope

For every child, gather

- Empty foil or plastic-wrap box, cut as shown (sketches a and b)
- Two 1½-inch (4-cm) square mirrors (available at craft supply stores)
- 2 corrugated cardboard pieces cut from pattern on p. 39
- Masking tape
- High-tack adhesive
- Rulers

introduce

If light travels in a straight line, is it possible to see around a corner? Let's make periscopes to find out!

Do

1. Use a ruler to fold and then tape corrugated pieces as shown (sketches c and d). Ask an adult if you need help.

2. Glue each mirror to the long side of each folded piece.

3. Cover any sharp cutting edges on your box with masking tape and tape the box lid firmly closed.

4. When mirrors are set, glue and set the mirrored triangles into box as shown. Tape box closed.

5. When glue is set, hold your periscope straight up. Look through one end. **Can you look over the top of something?**

6. Turn periscope sideways. **What do you have to do to look around a corner?**

a. cut 2" square / cut off flap / foil / cover serrated edge with tape

b. cut out 2" square

c. fold up to crease / cardboard strip / 1 1/2" mirror

d. tape ends together

e.

f. glue / glue / mirror / glue to box / glue to box

why it works

Because light travels in a straight line, we can make it turn a corner by reflecting it at an angle with a mirror. The mirror that is placed away from your eye reflects light from the object into the mirror placed next to your eye. That mirror reflects the light (and image) into your eye! This is how people in a submarine can see what is going on above the surface of the water.

Prayer and Praise

Periscopes' mirrors reflect things we can't see otherwise. **What else does light do for us?** Invite volunteers to finish this prayer: **Thank You, God, for light because . . .** (Optional: Students finish the prayer starter on individual papers, post papers and then read their prayers aloud by using their periscopes.)

Periscope
Pattern

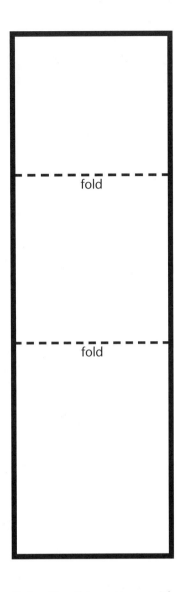

fold

fold

Note: Use this pattern with the instructions on page 38.

Seed Sprouter

For every four children, gather

- 4 small clear plastic containers (film container, bead container, etc.), each with a small hole drilled in lid
- 4 eye screws
- 8 to 12 seeds (bean, sunflower, etc.)
- Cotton balls
- Water in an open container
- Lengths of plastic lanyard
- Pony beads

introduce

Today we are going to make something that shows us how light energy can be turned into another kind of energy—plant energy!

Do

1. Screw the eye screw into the hole in the lid of your container.

2. Moisten two or more cotton balls with water.

3. Place cotton balls in your container and then slide a seed between each cotton ball and the outside of the container. Place the lid on the container.

4. Thread lanyard through the eye screw. Add pony beads as desired.

5. Tie lanyard and wear pendant or hang it in a well-lit place to see light energy become plant energy! Add water if needed to keep seeds moist. When sprouted, remove and plant the sprouts!

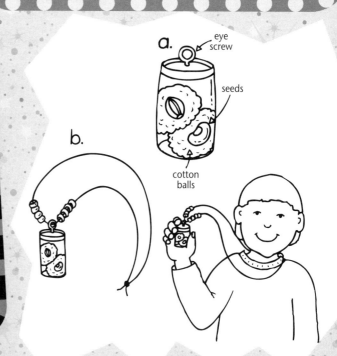

a. eye screw

seeds

b.

cotton balls

why it works

These seeds are moist, but what would happen if they didn't get light? (They would sprout, but would then die.) After seeds sprout, light energy turns into plant energy to keep the plant growing.

Prayer and Praise

What are some other reasons we need light? Students tell. What is your favorite reason to thank God for light? As I pray, add your reason to our prayer when I pause. Pray, pausing to allow volunteers to add their ideas. (Optional: Students write prayers of thanks in two ways: the first, without light—eyes closed; the second, with light—eyes open as they write.)

Elementary Experiments
DAY ONE: Light and Dark

Flash! Light

For every two children, gather
- 2 disposable light sticks or flashlights

introduce

God made the light. He also helps us use the light He made. Let's try this game!

Do

1. With your partner, agree on a signal using your light that will help you find each other in the dark (for example, turn on a flashlight to make a short flash and two long flashes at the ceiling; with a light stick, hold three fingers in front of it and then remove fingers one at a time, etc.).

2. When everyone is ready, darken the room as much as possible.

3. Move about the room, making your light signal from time to time. **Did you find your partner? Was it easy or difficult?**

4. Try it again with a different signal.

why it works

Besides making light for the planet, God also gave some creatures the ability to make and use chemical light (phosphorescence). Fireflies or lightning bugs have a chemical in their bodies with which they can make light to signal each other. Their light signals are very complex. Different kinds of fireflies have different signals so that they can communicate with each other.

Prayer and Praise

What are some ways we use light to communicate? (Stoplights. Flashing police or fire vehicle lights. Lighthouses. Fiber optic communication lines.) **Let's thank God for as many kinds of ways we communicate with lights as we can name.** Students say phrase or sentence prayers including their ideas. (Optional: Students draw their ideas and then show them before adding their ideas during prayer.)

DAY ONE: Light and Dark

Light colors

For every child, gather

- Flashlight
- 4-inch (10-cm) cellophane square in red, yellow or blue
- Rubber band

introduce

What color does red and blue make? Blue and yellow? Yellow and red? Children answer. Do colors of light combine in the same way as colors of pigments or paints? Let's experiment to see.

Do

1. Choose a color of cellophane. Secure the cellophane over the end of a flashlight with the rubber band.

2. Darken the room and shine your flashlight on the walls and ceilings. **What color do you see? Is the color the same everywhere you shine it?**

3. Try shining your light on the wall where the light of another person is shining. **What happens? What color did you see? Do the two colors combine to make the same color as when you combine the two colors of paint? Why or why not?**

why it works

Light is made up of waves. Every color in the spectrum has a different wavelength. When we see red paint, our eyes can tell it is red because the paint absorbs blue and yellow waves so red waves reflect to our eyes. But the colors of light are not absorbing any color, so they combine differently. All the colors of light our eyes are able to see can actually be made by combining blue, red and green light.

Prayer and Praise

What items do we see every day that combine colors of light? (Color TV. Computer screen.) **God made light in amazing ways.** Invite students to turn on flashlights and then briefly shine their lights onto another's light while volunteers take turns to say short prayers of thanks for light. (Optional: Children draw pictures of items that use colored light and add written prayers.)

DAY TWO

Sky and Water

"And God said, 'Let there be an expanse between the waters to separate water from water.' So God made the expanse and separated the water under the expanse from the water above it. And it was so. God called the expanse 'sky.' And there was evening, and there was morning—the second day."
Genesis 1:6-8

Here are experiments to help your kids understand the nature of Earth's atmosphere, kinds of weather and water!

DAY TWO: Sky and Water

Spray Paints

For every four children, gather

- Brightly colored crepe paper, cut or torn into bits
- White construction paper
- Small spray bottles filled with water
- Newspaper

introduce

Show several pieces of crepe paper. **What do you think water can do if we spray it on this colorful paper? Let's experiment to see what will happen!**

Do

1. Invite children to lay crepe-paper pieces onto white construction paper in any way they like and then spray water lightly over the crepe-paper pieces. **What do you see happening?**

2. Children spray more water as desired. **What happens now?**

3. Lay creations on newspaper to dry.

4. When paper is dry, children pull off crepe-paper pieces. **Where did the color from the crepe paper go?**

why it works

The crepe paper is full of tiny holes. The color is held in those tiny holes. When the water flows into those tiny holes, it washes out the color from the holes onto the white paper. Water moved the color onto your white papers.

Prayer and Praise

Think of one color on your picture. What does that color remind you of? Children respond. **Let's thank God for the colors He made. When I say your name, tell the color you thought of or what that color reminds you of. Dear God, (Keisha) is glad for (blue). It reminds (her) of the (sky).** (Optional: Children dictate prayers to be added to their crepe-paper prints.)

DAY TWO: Sky and Water

cartons of color

For every four children, gather

- Newspaper (spread over activity area)
- 2 to 4 white Styrofoam egg cartons
- Red, blue and yellow food coloring
- Cotton swabs
- Water in a cup

introduce

What is in these egg cartons? What colors do you see? What would happen if you mixed two of those colors?

Do

1. Ahead of time, add water to each section of egg cartons. Drop several drops of red food coloring into one section of each egg carton. Repeat in other sections with blue and yellow.

2. Children dip swabs into colored water and then swirl the swabs in the clear water sections to see the water change color. **Dip your swabs into other colors and then into water to make new colors.**

why it works

If we had dropped crayons into the water, would the crayons have colored the water? No. But food coloring is wet. We call that a liquid. Water is a liquid, too. Liquids mix together well.

Prayer and Praise

We mix many things in water. What are some of those things? (Drink mix. Bubble bath. Paint.) **Let's thank God for these ways we use water.** Children repeat prayer of thanks after you, phrase by phrase, inserting ideas as you point to volunteers. (Optional: Children paint with colored water on butcher paper. Add a written prayer and read it aloud.)

DAY TWO: Sky and Water

windy Race

For every four children, gather

• Long piece of butcher paper (with a lengthwise line drawn down the middle, and secured to table or floor with masking tape)

• Variety of lightweight items (cotton balls, leaves, feathers, etc.)

• Markers

• Straws

introduce

What have you seen blowing in the sky or across the top of water? Do you think that it is easier for the wind to blow a (feather) or to blow a (leaf)? Let's have a windy race to find out!

Do

1. Invite children to draw a start line and a finish line at either end of the paper.

2. Children use their straws to blow objects to the finish line.

3. Pairs blow items down either side of the line to compare. **Which item blows the farthest? Which is easiest or hardest to blow? Which item flies upward?**

why it works

When we blow through the straw, air is pushed out through a small space to make wind. The items move more easily if they are smooth. Air moves better over smooth items.

Prayer and Praise

When there is wind, what things blow around first? (Plastic bags. Leaves. Papers.) These things are light. God made wind to blow. Let's all stand in a line and make a big wind by blowing on our straws. Then we'll say together, "Thank You, God, for wind!"

wind watchers

For every four children, gather

- 4 paper plates
- Markers
- Scissors
- Crepe paper
- Masking tape or glue sticks

introduce

How can we tell when the weather is windy? Today we will make something that will help us tell when the wind is blowing.

Do

1. Invite children to decorate paper plates with the markers. **What can you draw to make a picture of a windy or cloudy day?**

2. Cut crepe paper into streamers. Help children tape or glue streamers to edges of plates.

3. Invite children to blow on the streamers. **What happens?** Children wave Wind Watchers to see the effects of moving air.

4. Take Wind Watchers outdoors and hold them still. **Is the wind blowing? How can you tell?**

5. Optional: Hang the Wind Watchers outdoors near a window so that children can see the streamers move in the wind.

why it works

When air gets warm, it rises, or goes up. That rising air "pulls" cooler air toward the warmer place. When air moves, it makes wind.

Prayer and Praise

When it is windy, do you feel warm or cold? (Usually, cold.) Let's pretend there is a cold wind blowing. Let's put on our coats. Pantomime putting on a coat. Let's put on our hats. Pantomime putting on a hat. Now hold on to your hats in the wind. Invite volunteers to say, Thank You, God, for the wind! (Optional: Children draw windy-day pictures and dictate a written prayer.)

wonderful waterfalls

For every four children, gather

- Sensory table or large pan containing sand, rocks and stones

- Sand tools

- Water in pitchers

- Optional—plastic tubes or pipes

introduce

What happens when we pour water down a hill? What could we build to stop water from flowing like a river? Do you think we can stop water? Let's find out!

Do

1. Children build dams, make pools and dig watercourses using rocks, sand and stones.

2. Children then pour water to watch it move through the watercourses. **How well do the dams and pools work to keep the water in one place? What might happen if the ponds or dams were lined with plastic sheeting?**

3. Optional: Children set the plastic tubes or pipes so that they can pour water through them. **How is this different from pouring water down a hill?**

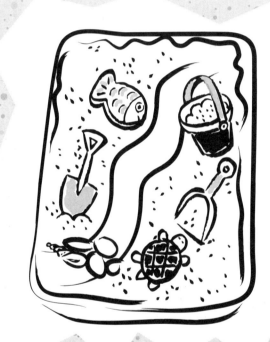

why it works

When we pour water, gravity pulls it downhill. The dams stop it for a little while but water finds the open spots and leaks out unless we put something waterproof in the way.

Prayer and Praise

What drinks do we drink? Children respond. **What do all those drinks contain? They all contain water! Let's thank God for as many kinds of drinks as we can.** Children take a turn to repeat a kind of drink as you pause in your prayer. (Optional: Children draw pictures of drinks with markers on a mural and then spray or paint water over the pictures to watch the colors change as you pray.)

Sensory Snow

For every four children, gather

- Plastic or real snow in a sensory table or large pan

- Tools for exploring snow (toy shovels, measuring cups, spoons, etc.)

- Optional—bagged ice (shaved or crushed), mittens, toy vehicles

introduce

When do you play in frozen water? What do we call frozen water that comes from the sky? Today we're going to see and feel what snow may be like!

Do

1. Children explore snow, using shovels, measuring cups, etc.

2. Optional: Add ice to snow and provide mittens for play.

3. Talk about snow's temperature and texture.

4. Optional: Add toy vehicles. Talk about what is different about the way they roll (and slide) on snow as compared to a dry surface.

why it works

God made many kinds of weather. When it gets cold enough to make water freeze, the water in the sky can freeze, too. Sometimes this water becomes snow. Sometimes it becomes hail. When hail or snowflakes get heavy enough, they fall to the ground.

Prayer and Praise

What are other kinds of weather? (Sunny. Warm. Rainy. Windy.) When I say your name, you can name one kind of weather. Pray, God, (Rena) thanks You for (rain). Repeat so each child has a turn. (Optional: Children act out the kind of weather chosen as you give each one a chance to insert an idea into the prayer.)

Early Childhood Explorations
DAY TWO: Sky and Water

icebergs

For every four children, gather

- Water table or dishpan half-filled with water
- Chunks of ice (freeze in plastic bags) and ice cubes
- Toy boats

introduce

In some parts of the ocean, the water is so cold that there are huge chunks of ice that never melt. They are called icebergs. Today we'll see how icebergs float.

Do

1. Place chunks of ice and ice cubes in water.

2. Children play with toy boats, moving them through the water around the ice. (Add more chunks of ice and ice cubes as needed.)

3. Look for the largest and smallest ice pieces. Are the ice pieces the same size as when they were put into the water? Is the water getting colder or warmer? Does most of an ice cube float on top of the water or below the surface of the water?

why it works

When a piece of ice floats in water, most of it floats under the top, or surface, of the water. This is what makes icebergs dangerous to boats. A person on a boat can only see the ice on top, not the ice under the water. Icebergs can break the parts of a boat that are underwater.

Prayer and Praise

When the ice melted in the water, what happened to the water? (It got colder.) **Let's thank God for making water and ice.** Invite children to clap softly whenever you say "water" and to shiver whenever you say "ice" as you pray. (Optional: Children drop dry tempera onto paper and use pieces of leftover ice to make paint. Put pictures on a bulletin board with "We thank God for ice and water!" lettered in the center.)

DAY TWO: Sky and Water

Bubble Blowers

For every four children, gather

• Dishpan containing bubble liquid (mix together ¼ cup liquid detergent [Dawn dishwashing liquid works best] and ¾ cup water)

• Bubble-blowing items (bubble wands, straws taped together, strawberry baskets, paper cups with holes poked in bottom, etc. If children use straws to blow bubbles, poke a hole near the top of each straw to keep solution from being sucked into mouths.)

introduce

Air is all around us. What part of your body has air in it? Let's blow bubbles to see!

Do

1. Children blow bubbles with different items. **What kinds of bubbles can you make? How do they look different? How can you blow bubbles with your hands?**

2. Compare sizes of bubbles. **Can you blow a bubble using all the air in your lungs? Can you blow a bubble using only a tiny puff of air? Which one is bigger?**

why it works

We cannot see air. But we can see that there is air in our lungs. When we blow the air out of our lungs at the bubble wand, the bubble liquid catches our air and holds it in for a little while. We can see that there is air in our lungs!

Prayer and Praise

What else can you do with the air in your lungs? (Breathe. Talk. Sing.) **Let's sing a song together to thank God for the air in our lungs.** Sing a song of thanks already familiar to children and add in **Jesus' name, amen.** (Optional: Children sing and illustrate a song of thanks to God on large butcher paper for a mural.)

DAY TWO: Sky and Water

water Fun

introduce

What can you do to make a jar of water full—without adding more water? Let's find out!

Do

1. Set jars on the tray and place a towel nearby.

2. Child chooses a jar. Children take turns to place one or more pebbles and rocks into jars. **How much does the water level change in your jar as a tiny pebble is added? How much does it change when a bigger rock is added?**

3. When the jar seems full, encourage children to try adding just one more pebble. **What happens? Can you add one more without the water spilling?**

why it works

When we add rocks, we can make the water come to the top of the jar. The rocks take up space where the water was before, so they push the water up out of the way. Even when the jar looks full, the water still can go a little higher. That's because the tiny bits of water (molecules) hold together for a little while (surface tension).

Prayer and Praise

What is a place where there is deep water? (Lake. Ocean.) A place where there is shallow water? (Creek. Stream.) **God made the water so that it flows into lakes and oceans. He made water so that we could live!** Ask a series of questions that can all be answered, "Water!" such as, "What makes plants grow?" and "What do I want when I'm thirsty?" Then invite children to end by saying, "God made water! Thank You, God!" (Optional: Children help you to spell out "thank you" with rocks as you talk and pray aloud.)

DAY TWO: Sky and Water

colorful Sights

For every eight children, gather

- Wide, clear container, half-filled with water
- Shaving cream
- Food coloring (primary colors)
- Eyedroppers

introduce

Do you think water is lighter or heavier than shaving cream? Let's try this to find out which is heavier.

Do

1. Set the container where children may easily observe it at eye level. Cover the surface of the water with a thick, even layer of shaving cream.

2. Children take turns using eyedroppers to insert and squirt several drops of food coloring into, but not through, the layer of shaving cream. Children watch at eye level as the food coloring (more dense than the water) drops through the shaving cream and spreads through the water.

3. Through a hole made by dropping one color, children squirt a second color fairly quickly. Color should follow the path of the first color to mix in the water with the first color. Repeat with other colors as interested.

why it works

The shaving cream is lighter (less dense) than the water. The food coloring is heavier (denser) than the water. Because the food coloring is heaviest, it falls through both the shaving cream and the water.

Prayer and Praise

What colors did we see? When are times we see those colors in the sky? God made beautiful colors in the sky for us to see. Let's thank Him for the colors. Invite each child to name a color and then close the prayer by thanking God for all the colors. (Optional: Take water and shaving cream mixture outdoors. Finger paint with mixture on cement and then thank God for colors.)

DAY TWO: Sky and Water

Water Filtering

For every four children, gather

- 2 clean jars with lids, one half-filled with water
- Soil
- Large spoon
- Clean sand
- 8-inch (20.5-cm) square of cheesecloth or cotton fabric
- Rubber band

Introduce

What do you think we can do to make dirty water clean? We're going to clean some dirty water today.

Do

1. Add some soil to the jar half-filled with water. I will help you screw the lid on tightly.

2. Take turns to shake the jar to make water muddy.

3. Lay the cloth over the opening of second jar, letting cloth sag down into the opening. I will help you put a rubber band around the cloth and jar.

4. Children take turns to spoon sand onto the cloth.

5. Pour the muddy water slowly through the sand. How does the water in the second jar look? Is it the same or different from the water in the first jar? What do you think is happening to change the water?

Why it works

The tiny pieces of dirt in the water are bigger than the spaces between the grains of sand. The bits of dirt get stuck in the sand, so the water comes out cleaner!

Prayer and Praise

Where do we get water to drink? (Tap. Bottle.) God gives us water to drink because He loves us and knows what we need! Let's thank Him for His love. After each sentence I pray, you may say, "Thank You, God, for loving me." Pray, allowing children to repeat their sentence between your sentences. (Optional: Children add a little water to unsweetened drink mix to make paint and then paint designs on large butcher paper. Write a prayer on the paper and then read it aloud, allowing children to respond as above.)

Surprise colors

For a large group, gather

- Plastic tray
- Variety of powdered fruit-flavored drinks
- Baking soda
- 2 to 4 eyedroppers
- Vinegar in a shallow container
- Optional—other liquids (water, milk, etc.) in shallow containers

introduce

Air is all around us, even though we can't see it. Air is made up of gases. Today we're going to make some gases to create a beautiful color surprise!

Do

1. Ahead of time, layer drink mix powders across the tray and then sprinkle baking soda over the drink powder to cover all color.

2. Children take turns to use eyedroppers to drop vinegar onto the baking soda. **What happens? Why? What colors appear?**

3. Optional: Try dropping other liquids on top of the baking soda. **What happens? What colors appear?**

why it works

When baking soda and vinegar touch each other, they react and make gas bubbles. The bubbles we made are colored because there is colored drink mix under the baking soda.

Prayer and Praise

God gives us air to breathe. He gives us colors to see. He made a beautiful world for us! Invite children to take turns to thank God for air, for colors or for our beautiful world. (Optional: Children draw pictures of the experiment and its colors as a way to thank God.)

Sunset Sky

For every four children, gather

- Small flashlight or penlight with black paper taped over its lighted end and a small hole made in paper to let light through

- Several glue sticks (for hot-glue guns)

- White paper or background

introduce

What color is the sky? When does the sky turn red, orange and yellow? Today we are going to find out why the sky is a different color at sunset and sunrise.

Do

1. One person may hold a glue stick over the hole in the paper at the end of your flashlight.

2. Another person may turn on the light while another person holds the paper near the flashlight.

3. Be sure everyone takes a turn to shine the flashlight at the paper. What color is the light as it goes into the glue stick? What color does it become as it shines out through the glue stick?

4. Hold a second glue stick next to the first one. Now take turns to shine the light through them as before. What do you notice about the color of the light as it goes into the second glue stick? What color shines on the paper? Why do you think the glue sticks change the color of the light?

5. Children may add more glue sticks as desired and then hold them while another shines the light. **What changes do you notice in the color of the light?**

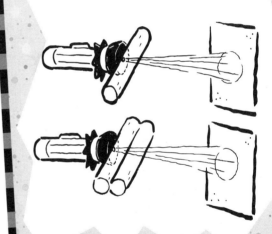

why it works

When the light travels through the glue sticks, the particles in the glue sticks scatter some colors of the light. The colors of light that are not scattered are red and yellow. At sunset, sunlight travels through more particles. This makes the sunset more red and yellow.

Prayer and Praise

What are some things that we see in the sky? Children respond. **God is good to make a beautiful sky for us! The Bible tells us that God said everything He made is good. Let's thank God for always loving us and making the world good. Let's say that together: "What God made is good."** Pray, pausing to let children insert "What God made is good" as you pray. (Optional: Children draw pictures of their experiments and dictate a prayer for an adult to write on his or her drawing.)

DAY TWO: Sky and Water

windy world

For every four children, gather
- Sheets of newspaper
- Lamp with exposed bulb
- Talcum powder

introduce

Do you know what causes the wind on our planet? Here's a good way to see how wind begins!

Do

1. *Teacher: Lay out the sheets of newspaper and set the lamp on the newspaper.*

2. Turn on the light. Let the bulb get warm.

3. Sprinkle some talcum powder into your hand. Drop it onto the light bulb. **What do you see?**

4. Try it again after you have turned off the light. **What happens? Why? Is the bulb warm or cool?**

why it works

Imagine that the earth is the light bulb. (But remember that Earth doesn't heat itself; the sun heats it.) As Earth heats up, it warms the air nearest to it. Since heat rises, the warm air moves up and away from the bulb. This lets cooler air rush in to take its place. This movement of warm and cold air is wind. Using the talcum powder helped you to see how the air moves.

Prayer and Praise

Which direction is the wind blowing today? Why do you think that is so? God set many natural laws in place so that the world would do everything He wanted it to. Write the letters of the word "WIND" down the middle of a large sheet of paper. Invite students to write or suggest words that begin with or contain those letters to create an acrostic prayer of thanks to God. (Optional: Students draw a mural illustrating causes and effects of wind, adding a written prayer to mural.)

DAY TWO: Sky and Water

Baking-Soda Bubbles

For every four children, gather

- ¼ cup baking soda in a small clear cup

- 1 cup vinegar in cup

- Container of bubble solution with wand (available from toy stores; optional—a "bubble gun," also available from toy stores)

- Large clear plastic bowl

introduce

The Bible says that God separated the waters above (sky) from waters below (seas). This experiment will help us understand how God did that!

Do

1. Set the baking soda cup in the clear bowl.

2. Pour the vinegar over it and watch the reaction make carbon dioxide bubbles.

3. Use the bubble wand to blow bubble solution bubbles into the baking soda and vinegar bubbles. (Optional: Blow bubbles with bubble gun.) **What happens?**

why it works

The carbon dioxide inside the baking-soda-and-vinegar bubbles is denser than air. ("Denser" means the molecules are closer together.) Those bubbles stay at the bottom of the bowl. The air in the bubbles you blew is less dense than carbon dioxide, so the air bubbles float above the carbon dioxide bubbles.

Prayer and Praise

How do you think this experiment might help us understand why the sky and water can be separated? (Some things God made are denser than others. Some gases float above others.) **Let's name some other things that float.** Invite a volunteer to pray, thanking God for one or more of the items mentioned. (Optional: Students illustrate the experiment and add written prayers of thanks.)

Dense Doings

For every four children, gather

• 5 plastic cups, each containing about 4 ounces (.12 l) of one of the following liquids: light corn syrup, glycerin, water, cooking oil, rubbing alcohol

• Liquid food coloring (can be shared among groups)

• Craft sticks

• Pencil and paper

• Tall clear jar or glass

introduce

The molecules in water are closer together, or denser, than the molecules in air. Let's see how density works. Which liquid do you think will be on top?

Do

1. *Teacher: Tell students what each liquid is.*

2. As your teacher tells what each liquid is, write down its name. Squirt a little food coloring into each liquid and stir with a craft stick.

3. Write down the color you added beside each liquid's name to help you remember which is which.

4. Take turns to tilt the jar and then pour each liquid carefully into the jar so liquid runs down the inside without mixing too much.

4. Watch the filled jar. **What happens to each colored liquid? Why?**

5. Look at the notes you made about the colors. **Which liquid is densest? Which is least dense?**

6. If you have time, stir the liquids and then watch what happens!

why it works

The atmosphere of our planet is a lot like the layers of liquids in our jars. The liquids at the bottom are densest. Their molecules are closer together. Even though each group colored their liquids differently, the same liquid is at the bottom of each jar.

Prayer and Praise

God created a layer of air that is just perfect for us to breathe! It is less dense than water. It is denser than the gases in the upper atmosphere. Let's thank God for our atmosphere. (Optional: Students draw a mural illustrating layers of atmosphere and write prayers of thanks to God on mural.)

Salty Floaters

For every four children, gather

- Tall clear glass nearly filled with water
- Section of carrot smaller than the diameter of the cup
- Container of salt and a spoon

introduce

Is it easier to float in ocean water or in lake water? Why? Try this experiment to see!

Do

1. Drop the section of carrot into the water. **What happens?**

2. Now add salt, a spoonful at a time. After you've added some salt, stop to notice what is happening to the carrot. **Why do you think this is happening?**

3. Add more salt. **What can you do to make the carrot rise to the top of the glass?**

why it works

Adding salt to water makes the water denser. The carrot then has more molecules supporting it, so it floats higher and higher in the glass. In the same way, salt water in oceans is denser than fresh water in lakes. You can float more easily in the ocean than in a lake.

Prayer and Praise

What do you think might have happened to make the oceans salty? (Minerals and salt flow down rivers into oceans. Ocean water evaporates to make rain, leaving more minerals and salt in oceans.) **God made everything in perfect balance! Let's thank God for as many different bodies of water as we can.** Volunteers pray aloud, each naming a kind of body of water. (Optional: Students create a 3-D map from flour and salt dough, illustrating various bodies of water and adding written prayers.)

DAY TWO: Sky and Water

Self-watering Seed Starter

For every child, gather

- 2-liter soda bottle, cut as shown
- Water with food coloring added
- Paper towels
- Slightly moistened potting soil with scoop
- Seeds for sprouting (beans, alfalfa, grass, etc.)

introduce

Which direction does water usually flow? Today we'll find a way to make water move uphill so that it waters seeds!

Do

1. Tightly roll up a paper towel.

2. Turn the bottle top upside down like a funnel. Slide the rolled towel into the bottle's neck.

3. If the roll slides out, stuff more paper towel around it to tighten.

4. Fill the funnel part with moist potting soil. Push seeds into the soil next to the sides so you can see the seeds grow!

5. Fill the bottom of the bottle about ⅓ full of water.

6. Set your soil-filled funnel on top so that the end of the towel roll touches the water. Watch the towel roll. **What happens?**

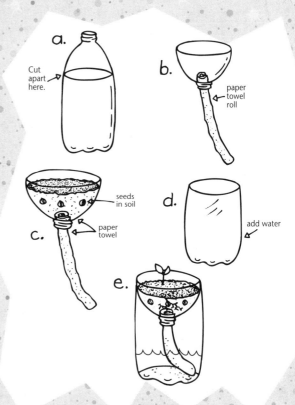

a. Cut apart here.

b. paper towel roll

c. seeds in soil / paper towel

d. add water

e.

why it works

If you keep water in the bottom of your bottle, the paper towel will move water up into the soil to keep it moist. This is called capillary action. You see, water molecules stick to each other. So when the towel touches the water, the water molecules pull each other upward! Capillary action also moves moisture up through the roots, stems and leaves of plants so that they can grow and make food for us.

Prayer and Praise

God provides everything we need to live! Let's name as many ways as we can think of to use water. Volunteers tell; then thank God for some of the ways listed. (Optional: Students paint watercolor illustrations of ways they use water daily and add written prayers.)

DAY TWO: Sky and Water

tornado in a Bottle

For every child, gather

- 2 soda bottles (labels removed)
- Duct tape or electrical tape
- Pencil
- Water in a pitcher
- Glitter or bits of grass

introduce

What does a tornado look like? A tornado makes the fastest wind on Earth. Near the vortex (center) of it, wind may blow at over 200 miles per hour! Let's discover how a tornado behaves.

Do

1. Put tape firmly over the mouth and neck of one bottle.

2. Use the pencil to make a pencil-sized hole in the tape over the bottle mouth.

3. Fill the second bottle nearly full with water. Add glitter or grass.

4. Turn the empty bottle upside down. Tightly tape its mouth over the mouth of the bottle holding water. Use more tape to seal it and support the neck.

5. Now turn the whole thing upside down. Move it around to start the water swirling. Watch to see how the shape of the vortex changes. **Where does the glitter or grass go? How is this like a real tornado?**

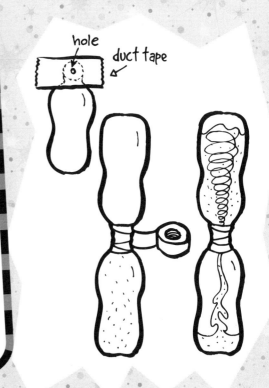

hole

duct tape

why it works

A tornado moves like the water in your bottles. When weather conditions are right, the wind in a thunderstorm changes direction. It gets stronger as it rises, which creates a rotating column of air. This column (funnel) may not extend to Earth's surface. But when it does, what happens looks a lot like what happened inside your bottles!

Prayer and Praise

Psalm 46:1 says that God is our refuge and strength. Even in a tornado, we can remember that we belong to God, who made this amazing weather! When are times God kept you safe? Let's thank God for His power and His protection. (Optional: Students draw pictures of different kinds of weather on large butcher paper, adding the words of Psalm 46:1.)

Elementary Experiments
DAY TWO: Sky and Water

water wonder

For every four children, gather

- Dishpan
- Pitcher of water
- 4 water glasses
- 4 to 8 large index cards

introduce

Have you ever tried to turn a glass of water upside down? What happened? Try this way to turn a glass of water upside down!

Do

1. Fill your glass to the very top with water. Make sure the rim is wet.

2. Slide the index card over the top of the glass.

3. Hold the card in place and flip the glass upside down over the dishpan.

4. Wait a moment and then remove your hand. **What is happening? Why?**

why it works

There is air pressure all around us. This pressure pushes up on the index card as the water in the upside-down glass pushes down. The pressure holds the card still for a little while. When water begins to seep out, air begins to rush into the glass. The air pushes out the rest of the water and gravity pulls the water downward so that it falls.

Prayer and Praise

God created us to live at the bottom of an ocean of air just as He created fish to live in an ocean of water. Air pushes into our lungs just as it pushes the card up against the water! What else do we need to live? Let's thank God for these things. If you volunteered something we need to live, say it again when I pause. Pray, thanking God for air and pausing for volunteers to add their ideas. (Optional: Students make a mural by blowing paint with straws and adding written prayers.)

DAY TWO: Sky and Water

Air Force!

For every four children, gather

- 2 potatoes

- 8 to 10 sturdy straight plastic drinking straws (if using inexpensive straws, have extras available)

introduce

Air is everywhere around Earth. How strong do you think a column of air could be? Let's try this experiment to find out!

Do

1. With one hand on the potato, hold a straw near its top. Place the other end of the straw against the potato. **Can you push the end of the straw into the potato? What happens?**

2. Take another straw. Seal the top end of the straw with your thumb. Try to push the end of the straw into the potato again. **What happened? Why do you think it happened?**

3. Take turns to try this more times. **Does it always work the same way? Why?**

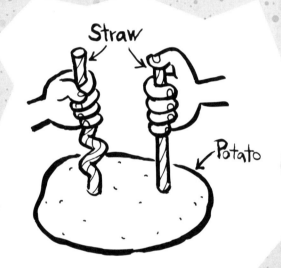

Straw

Potato

why it works

The open straw didn't get very far into the potato. But what happened with the closed straw? The air inside the straw was trapped by your thumb and compressed between your thumb and the potato. This made the closed straw strong enough to drill into the potato. The compressed air inside kept the straw from bending.

Prayer and Praise

Many power tools use compressed air in just this way. Pneumatic drills use compressed air to break hard substances like rock. What are some other ways we use air? (Fans. Hair and clothes dryers.) Let's thank God for ways we can use air! Students take turns to say sentence prayers, including their ideas. (Optional: Students use straws to make blow paintings, adding written prayers.)

DAY TWO: Sky and Water

thin-Skinned water

For every child, gather

- Plastic or paper bowl half-filled with water
- 3 toothpicks
- A shallow container with a small amount of dish detergent

introduce

Water has many amazing characteristics. Today we're going to see how water molecules hold on to each other!

Do

1. Lay two toothpicks beside each other in the water. **What do they do?**

2. With a third toothpick, pick up a drop of dish detergent.

3. Touch the soapy toothpick tip between the floating toothpicks. **What happens?**

why it works

Water molecules hold on to each other. Some people call them "sticky" molecules. Because of the way the molecules hold together, the surface of the water in your cup acts as if it has a thin skin on top. This is called surface tension. It allows the toothpicks to float on top. When the dish detergent touches the water, it breaks the molecular bonds of the surface. The water molecules move outward and take the floating sticks with them!

Prayer and Praise

What would our clothes look like if we washed them only in water? What other things do we use soap or detergent to wash? (Dishes. Cars.) Invite several volunteers to pray, thanking God for ways we use water, besides drinking it. (Optional: Students draw pictures of ways we use water and then add written prayers to their papers.)

DAY TWO: Sky and Water

Rainmaker

For every four children, gather

- Metal pie tin
- Jar
- Thermal carafe of hot water
- Ice cubes

introduce

Have you ever wondered what makes rain happen? Let's try this experiment to find out how rain is made.

Do

1. Fill the pie tin with ice cubes. Wait for the tin to become very cold.

2. Pour hot water into your jar (or ask an adult to do it).

3. Set the ice-filled pie tin on top of the jar of hot water.

4. Watch. **What do you see inside the jar?**

5. After several minutes, lift the pie tin to look at its bottom. **What is on the bottom of the tin?** Tilt the pan so that the drops fall into the jar. You've made rain!

why it works

The water in the jar was hot. It gave off steam (or vapor). Since heat rises, the vapor rose until it hit the cold layer (the pie tin). Cold turns the vapor back into a liquid (condensation). When these water drops get too heavy, they fall. On Earth, the principle is the same: When warmed by the sun, water vapor rises. It hits colder air, condenses and then falls as rain!

Prayer and Praise

One of God's great gifts to Earth is the way He made the water cycle. How does rain help living things? (Makes plants grow. Keeps us alive.) What do you like best about rain? Let's thank God while we make the sound of rain with our fingers. Students tap open palms to make rain sounds as volunteers thank God for rain. (Optional: Students form teams; each team draws a step in the water cycle. Post pictures in order and add a written prayer to make a bulletin board display.)

DAY TWO: Sky and Water

Electricity Everywhere

For every four children, gather

- Tissue paper
- Hole punch
- Small round balloon
- Optional—salt and pepper

Introduce

God made lightning. What is lightning? Students respond. Besides lightning in the sky, electricity is everywhere. We're going to prove it!

Do

1. Use the hole punch to make tissue-paper circles. Place circles on a table.

2. Blow up the balloon until it is fairly tight.

3. Rub the balloon against a person's hair or a carpet at least 10 times.

4. Hold the rubbed side of the balloon a few inches above the tissue-paper circles. **What happens?**

5. Optional: Try rubbing the balloon and then holding it over salt and pepper scattered on the table. **What happens?**

Why it works

When we rub the balloon, it excites the electrons (charged particles on the outside of atoms). The electrons move from the hair or carpet to the balloon. That creates an electric charge on the balloon. The charge attracts the paper circles (or the pepper).

Prayer and Praise

What would your house be like if no one had ever discovered how to use electricity? Invite volunteers to thank God for a way we use electricity every day. (Optional: Students draw pictures of life without electricity and add a written prayer.)

icy and immiscible

For every four children, gather

- 4 clear plastic cups, half-filled with vegetable oil

- 4 colored ice cubes (add food coloring to water before freezing cubes)

introduce

Oil and water don't mix. But both ice and oil float on top of water. When they are together, which one will stay floating on top? Let's find out!

Do

1. Gently place your ice cube into the cup of oil. **Does it sink or float?**

2. **What happens if you blow your warm breath on the ice cube or hold the cup in your warm hands?** Try it to see.

3. **What do you think will happen as the ice melts completely?** After the ice melts, compare your prediction (what you expected) with your observation (what you saw).

why it works

As long as it is ice, the frozen water floats because it is less dense. But when the ice begins to melt, it becomes denser as it becomes water. Water is denser than oil and has very different molecular bonds from oil. Those very different bonds keep the substances from mixing.

Prayer and Praise

God created many things that we cannot see—things like molecular bonds. What are some other things we don't see but that are part of our lives? Students tell. (Electricity. Gravity.) **Let's thank God for the amazing way He made our world.** Volunteers pray sentence prayers that include one or more of the ideas students gave. (Optional: Students make sculptures from dough that remind them of things they don't see but that are part of their lives; students show and describe finished sculptures and pray.)

DAY TWO: Sky and Water

Personal Windpower

For every child, gather

- 9-inch (23-cm) square of paper
- Scissors
- Tape
- Push pin
- Drinking straw

introduce

What effects of wind do we often see? What are some things we use wind to do? Students respond. **Is it simple or difficult to make a windmill? Let's try it!**

Do

1. Fold your piece of paper in half to make a triangle.

2. Fold it in half the other way to make a triangle. Unfold the paper.

3. See where the lines cross? That's the center of your windmill.

4. Cut about halfway down each fold line. Then tape the tips of every other point together at the center of the paper.

5. Push the push pin through the center in the front and then push the straw onto the back side (point) of the push pin. You've got a windmill! Test by blowing to find out what the best angle is for the windmill to move. Take your windmill outside. **Where does it work best?**

Push Pin

Straw

why it works

The force of the moving air catches the edges of the windmill and rotates it. A windmill uses the force of wind (moving air) to power a machine, or else it stores that energy to turn into electricity. Our windmills aren't attached to machines but they work the same way!

Prayer and Praise

What is another way you might use the wind? (Kiting. Sailing.) **We use the wind in many ways every day. Let's thank God for the power He shows in His creation.** Pray, pausing after each phrase for students to say, "Thank You, God, for Your power." (Optional: Students write words of praise on their windmills and read them aloud as part of a prayer.)

DAY THREE

Dry Ground and Plants

"And God said, 'Let the water under the sky be gathered to one place, and let dry ground appear.' And it was so. God called the dry ground 'land,' and the gathered waters he called 'seas.' And God saw that it was good. Then God said, 'Let the land produce vegetation: seed-bearing plants and trees on the land that bear fruit with seed in it, according to their various kinds.' And it was so. The land produced vegetation: plants bearing seed according to their kinds and trees bearing fruit with seed in it according to their kinds. And God saw that it was good. And there was evening, and there was morning—the third day."

Genesis 1:9-13

Welcome to a variety of earth- and plant-science explorations and experiments!

DAY THREE: Dry Ground and Plants

Branches for Brushes

For every four children, gather

- Variety of small leafy twigs or branches
- Tempera paint in shallow containers
- Construction paper
- Optional—pine twigs, strings, other tree materials

introduce

What do we usually use to paint on paper? Today we are going to explore using something that comes from trees to paint on paper!

Do

1. Invite children to dip branch paintbrushes in paint and paint on construction paper.

2. Optional: Tie several small pine twigs together to make a paintbrush. Provide other items from trees (acorns, cones, bark, etc.) for children to dip into paint and then print on paper.

why it works

God made every kind of tree to have different leaves. God made some leaves long and skinny. He made some leaves round or feathery. How many shapes of leaves have we painted with today?

Prayer and Praise

Trees do a very important job. Besides giving us fruit and shade, they make the air cleaner and better every single day! What kinds of tree branches did we use today? Let's thank God for different kinds of trees. Volunteers take turns to name a kind of tree already mentioned as you pause during prayer. Close by saying, **Thank You, God, for trees that make good air!** (Optional: Children dictate prayers of thanks to add to their tree-branch paintings.)

DAY THREE: Dry Ground and Plants

Leaf inspectors

For every four children, gather

- Variety of leaves
- Paper and crayons
- Optional—magnifying glasses

introduce

God made many kinds of leaves. Today we're going to be leaf scientists. We'll look at leaves to help us play a game, and then we'll make rubbings to help us see parts of the leaves.

Do

1. Each child selects a leaf and examines it. **What color is it? What is different about your leaf?**

2. After inspecting leaves, children mix everyone's leaves together. **See if you can find your first leaf.**

3. Lay your leaf under a sheet of paper. Color the paper over the leaf with a crayon. (The side of the crayon works best.) **What part of the leaf shows most?**

4. Optional: Children use magnifying glasses to examine leaves and sort them by size, color, shape or texture.

why it works

Looking carefully at something is an important part of being a scientist. Looking at your leaf helped you to remember what it looked like. Making a rubbing helped you see the veins in the leaves. The veins carry the water and minerals from the roots of the plant to every cell in the leaves.

Prayer and Praise

What do you think leaves do? (Give shade. Make food for plant.) **Leaves also help to make the air better and cleaner. Let's thank God for leaves!** Invite children to wave their leaves in the air as they repeat phrase-by-phrase. **Dear God, thank You for leaves. We are glad for good air. We are glad for the shade. We are glad for the food plants make for us to eat. In Jesus' name, amen.** (Optional: Children glue leaves to papers to make leaf displays. Add a written prayer that you read aloud together.)

DAY THREE: Dry Ground and Plants

Bean Sorting

For every four children, gather

- Variety of types of beans in a shallow pan
- Paper plates
- Measuring cups and spoons

Introduce

God made many kinds of plants. Some of those plants make seeds we can eat! What kinds of beans have you eaten? Let's sort these beans. Then we can count them to find out which type of bean has the most.

Do

1. Invite children to find and lay one of each type of bean onto a different paper plate.

2. Children examine, scoop and pour beans with the measuring cups and spoons as they sort beans onto plates holding a matching bean.

3. Encourage children to estimate which type of bean has the largest pile.

4. Count the beans on each plate. **Which plate has the most? Which beans are largest? Smallest? Plain? Speckled? Dark-colored? Light-colored?**

Why it works

God made many kinds of beans—many more kinds than we have here. He gave us eyes to see the different kinds and hands to be able to separate them.

Prayer and Praise

What is a food your family likes to eat? What kinds of beans do you eat? What is a food you like to share with your friends? Let's thank God for these good foods. Invite volunteers to say sentence prayers of thanks for food. (Optional: Children share a snack while talking about food and then pray after eating.)

DAY THREE: Dry Ground and Plants

Grain Grind

introduce

One of the reasons God made plants is to give us food to eat! Today we are going to try grinding grain into smaller pieces to cook or to bake into bread.

Do

1. Ahead of time, post a note alerting parents to the use of food in this activity. Also check registration forms for possible food allergies.

2. Pour grain into each pie plate. Show children how to press firmly while twisting stones over grain to break into smaller pieces. **Do you think it is easy or hard to do?**

3. Optional—Children look at the pieces of ground-up grain with a magnifying glass. **How do the grains look different now?**

4. Optional—After children's grain is ground as fine as possible, dump all pie tins of grain together into a large bowl. Invite children to sprinkle a little salt over the flour. Add a little oil with the water and let children mix into a soft dough. With adult help, children take turns to make balls of dough, flatten them and then cook small flatbreads in electric skillet. (Add flour to the grain dough if needed.)

why it works

Grain can be eaten whole. Whole grains take longer to cook. So when they are broken up, the smaller pieces cook faster.

Prayer and Praise

What grains do we eat whole? (Rice. Hominy.) **What grains do we eat popped?** (Popcorn.) **What grains do we usually eat ground into flour?** (Wheat. Rye.) **Let's thank God for grain. You may choose the kind of grain for which you want to thank God.** Children take turns to name a grain as you pause during your prayer. (Optional: Children draw pictures of kinds of grain-based foods they like to eat. Add dictated prayers of thanks.)

DAY THREE: Dry Ground and Plants

Earthy Folks

For every four children, gather

- Sturdy paper plates
- Nature objects (sticks, leaves, rocks, pinecones, etc.)
- Glue
- Construction paper, cut into circles, squares, triangles, etc.
- Scissors, markers

introduce

God made wonderful rocks and plants. Today we'll use some of the things God made to make little people shapes.

Do

1. Invite children to gather sticks, rocks and leaves on paper plates and arrange materials into shapes like bodies.

2. Children draw a face, hands or feet on construction-paper shapes and glue shapes where desired.

3. What is your person made from? What is your person's name? What do you think your person does all day?

why it works

We used rocks and sticks to make shapes like people. But God uses rocks and plants to make more soil! Rocks are broken down into bits very slowly by the weather and wind. Parts of trees die and fall to the ground. The dead branches and seeds are broken down by the weather, too. They become part of the soil.

Prayer and Praise

Why are we glad that God made soil? (Grows plants so we can eat.) Children take turns to hold up their people sculptures and say, "God made soil!" Close by saying, **Thank You, God, for soil so that we can grow food!** (Optional: Children dictate prayers of thanks to be written on the paper plates that hold their people sculptures.)

DAY THREE: Dry Ground and Plants

Dirt Fun

For every four children, gather

- Dirt (outdoors)
- Hand trowels and paper cups
- Paper plates, plastic knives and spoons
- Microscope or magnifying glasses
- Poster board and marker
- Optional—planting mix, seeds, water

Introduce

What do people use dirt for? What do you think we can find in dirt if we look carefully?

Do

1. Take children outdoors to dig with hand trowels and collect dirt in paper cups.

2. Indoors, children dump soil onto paper plates and then use plastic utensils and microscope or magnifying glasses to examine soil.

3. On poster board, print each child's name. Record children's remarks about what was observed in the soil.

4. Optional: After exploration, children add all soils to planting mix. Invite children to plant seeds in their paper cups, water seeds and watch them grow!

Why it works

God made dirt. It is a wonderful thing! Dirt is made up of many tiny bits of rock, bits of dead plants and other things. Dirt gives plants things they need to grow. And when plants grow, we have food to eat!

Prayer and Praise

What food have you seen growing in dirt in a field or garden? God is good to give us everything we need. Let's thank God for good food. Children take turns to name a food. Close by saying, **Thank You, God, for food and plants!**

(Optional: Children draw and dictate information about what they found in the soil. Invite them to add words or letters they know and add a written prayer.)

Fruit Boats

For every four children, gather

- 4 grapefruit and/or orange halves with insides removed
- Dishpan half-filled with water
- 4 spoons
- Paper towels

Introduce

Where do oranges and grapefruit grow? What does a tree need for growing fruit? A tree needs water to grow fruit. How much water do you think it takes to fill half a (grapefruit)? Let's find out!

Do

1. Ahead of time, post a note alerting parents to the use of food in this activity. Also check registration forms for possible food allergies.

2. Children float grapefruit and orange halves in dishpan, like boats. **What happens as you place spoonfuls of water in fruit boats?** Use paper towels to clean up spills.

3. When fruit halves are full of water, children take them out of dishpan. Using the same spoon, children take the water out, counting the number of spoonfuls of water removed from each fruit half.

4. Use the fruit scooped out from the halves with other fruit to make a snack.

why it works

When we put enough water into our fruit boats, what happened? When there is water inside the boat, it makes the boat as heavy as the water. It sinks down. How many spoonfuls of water did you take out of your fruit half? A tree needs a lot of water to grow fruit!

Prayer and Praise

What words could you use to tell about our fruit boats? (Round. Smooth. Shiny. Nice smell. Yellow. Orange. White.) Pray a prayer of thanks to God, using as many descriptive words as your children gave. (Optional: Children tear and rub fruit peels onto paper to smell them. Thank God for the scent when you pray.)

Seed Match

For a large group, gather

- Variety of fruit and vegetable seeds (apple, watermelon, squash, peach, corn, tomato, cucumber, etc.)
- Knife (for adult)
- Glue
- Resealable plastic bags
- Marker

introduce

God made all kinds of foods for us to eat. The food and water God gives us shows His love for us. Let's look inside some fruits and vegetables.

Do

1. Ahead of time, post a note alerting parents to the use of food in this activity. Also check registration forms for possible food allergies.

2. Cut fruits and vegetables in half. From one half, extract seeds. Glue seeds to an index card. Place other half of item with seeds intact inside a resealable plastic bag and seal bag.

3. Invite children to examine the fruit and vegetable halves in bags and name each one. Children then match seeds and fruit. **Is it easy or hard to match the seeds to the fruit or vegetable the seeds came from?**

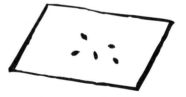

why it works

The fruits and vegetables have many seeds. When we look at the fruits and vegetables carefully, we notice the shape, size and color of the seeds. God gave us eyes and hands so that we can match them to the seeds on the cards.

Prayer and Praise

What foods do you eat that are made from (apples)? Repeat question for several of the foods you brought. **Where do (apples) come from? I'm glad God made (apples).** Let's each take a turn to say, "I'm glad God made (name of a fruit or vegetable)." Close by saying, **Thank You, God, for seeds that make fruit and vegetables grow!** (Optional: Children eat fruit and vegetable samples and then use seeds to plant.)

When Does it Grow?

For every four children, gather

- Variety of winter vegetables (sweet potatoes, cabbage, white potatoes, gourds, pumpkins, squashes, etc.)

- Knife (for adult)

Introduce

Some plants grow vegetables that are ready to eat during the summer. Some plants grow food that is not ready to eat until the fall, when it begins to get cold. Let's look at some colder-weather vegetables.

Do

1. Ahead of time, post a note alerting parents to the use of food in this activity. Also check registration forms for possible food allergies.

2. Invite children to explore the vegetables, naming, touching and holding them. Compare. **Which one is heaviest? Lightest? Biggest? Smallest? Which one is most colorful?**

3. Cut vegetables in half and let children touch and smell them.

4. Children help prepare and serve a snack made from one of the vegetables (pumpkin pie, baked squash or potatoes, etc.).

Why it Works

These foods that are ripe in the fall are called "winter vegetables" because people eat them during the winter. Many years ago, there were no refrigerators. People stored these kinds of vegetables in holes or cellars in the ground so that they would have food to eat during the winter.

Prayer and Praise

God loves us so much that He doesn't give us food only in the summer. He gives us food in the fall and winter, too! Invite volunteers to name one of the vegetables as you pause in a prayer of thanks to God. (Optional: Children use cut sections of the vegetables to make paint prints. Add a written prayer for a fall bulletin board display.)

DAY THREE: Dry Ground and Plants

Bag Biome

For every child, gather

- Lower half of a 2-liter soda bottle
- Gallon-sized resealable storage bag
- Pebbles
- Potting soil
- Seeds
- Water

introduce

A biome is a place like a forest or prairie where the plants and animals live together. Do you think we could build biomes? Let's try!

Do

1. Child pours an inch of pebbles into the bottom of bottle half.

2. Child pours about twice as much potting soil as pebbles into the bottle half.

3. Child pushes a little furrow in the soil with fingers about as deep as fingernails.

4. Child sprinkles seeds in the furrow and pushes soil over the seeds.

5. Child pours water into biome until water collects in the pebbles.

6. Child puts the biome into the bag and seals the bag.

7. Child sets the biome in a sunny place. **Watch to see the plants grow!**

Potting Soil

Pebbles

why it works

The things a plant needs to grow are all contained in your biome—soil, water, air and light. Check your biome every day. The water will move out of the soil and make rain. Soon you will see your seeds sprout!

Prayer and Praise

Plants need sunlight, soil, water and air to grow. What do we need to grow? (Food. Water. Homes. Rest. Love.) Let's thank God for making what we need to grow! Invite children to repeat this prayer, clapping along with you: **Thank You, God, for rest and home. Thank You, God, for helping us grow. Thank You, God, Your world is good. You love us and You give us food.**

DAY THREE: Dry Ground and Plants

Magnetic Food

For every four children, gather

- 4 sandwich-sized resealable bags
- Iron-fortified dry cereal
- 4 strong bar magnets

introduce

When plants grow grain, we make the grain into cereal. But there is something else in this cereal. We will use magnets to find it!

Do

1. Instruct each child to fill a bag about half full with dry cereal.

2. Using their hands, children gently crush the cereal inside the bag until it is in tiny pieces.

3. Children slowly move the end of a magnet across the outside of the bag. **What do you see happening?**

why it works

Iron is a kind of metal that is important for us to get into our bodies. So that we get enough, some kinds of cereals have iron added to them. Iron is also the metal that is attracted to magnets. So when we slowly move the magnets over our bags, we can see the tiny bits of iron move to cling to our magnets!

Prayer and Praise

What is your favorite kind of cereal? Volunteers tell. Invite volunteers to thank God for favorite cereals or for iron. (Optional: Children glue remaining cereal onto butcher paper and then dictate prayers of thanks to add to paper.)

DAY THREE: Dry Ground and Plants

Plant Smelling

For every four children, gather

- Variety of plant parts (flowers, leaves, seeds, cones, twigs, etc.) from different plants (include some strongly-scented plants like pine, cedar, alder, etc.)

- Paper lunch bags

Introduce

How do flowers smell? Do you think other parts of plants have a smell? Do all plants smell the same? Let's use our noses to be plant detectives!

Do

1. Children explore plant parts. **Which ones are soft? Spiky? Hard? Brittle?**

2. Children crush or roll plant parts to release the scent of each plant. **Describe how each one smells. Does it smell sweet? Spicy?**

3. Children place a crushed part from each plant in a separate bag, close the bag and leave a matching plant part to the ones in the bags out on a table.

4. Children take turns to close eyes, open a bag and then sniff. With eyes closed, they find the plant on the table that matches by smell.

why it works

Every plant has its own scent. Even the parts that are not flowers have a smell. Those smells help insects know what kind of plant they are on. When you walk on freshly-mowed grass or walk through pine woods, you can smell the different smells of the plants, too.

Prayer and Praise

How many flowers can you name? (Rose. Daisy. Sunflower.) Let's thank God for all the flowers we can name. We'll all say, "Thank You, God, for (child says flower name)." (Optional: Children glue plant parts to paper to make designs. Add a dictated prayer.)

juice Stop

For every four children, gather

- Variety of fruits and vegetables cut into wedges or chunks

- Matching juices (tomato and tomato juice, orange and orange juice, apple and apple juice, etc.)

- Paper cups, plates, napkins

- Paper and marker

introduce

Today we are going to be plant detectives. When you taste the juice, see if you can tell which fruit or vegetable it came from.

Do

1. Ahead of time, post a note alerting parents to the use of food in this activity. Also check registration forms for possible food allergies.

2. Ahead of time, set out chunks of fruit and vegetables on paper plates. Set plates on table and pour sample amounts of juices into cups.

3. Invite children to taste different juices and then try to match the juice to its fruit or vegetable. **To help match the fruit or vegetable to the juice, taste the wedges and chunks of fruit and vegetables. How are they alike? How do they taste different?**

why it works

Juice is one way we can save a fruit or vegetable for later. When fruit and vegetable juices are frozen or canned, we can keep them much longer than we could keep a fresh fruit or vegetable.

Prayer and Praise

What are other ways we eat fruit and vegetables? (Dried. Frozen. Cooked. Canned.) **God loves us! He gives us good food. When we pray, I will stop so you can say the name of your favorite food.** (Optional: Children draw pictures of their favorite foods and then dictate prayers of thanks.)

DAY THREE: Dry Ground and Plants

Pud talk

For every four children, gather

- Box of cornstarch
- 2 shallow baking pans
- 2 cups water

introduce

Who here has been to the beach? What happens to the sand when the waves move over your feet? Today we are going to make a funny mixture called pud. It acts a little like sand does when it is full of water.

Do

1. Child pours half a box of cornstarch into a shallow baking pan.

2. Another child slowly adds one cup of water (half of the 2-cup container). Children take turns stirring mixture to the consistency of pudding. (Adjust water and cornstarch ratios as needed.)

3. Children repeat the process to make another batch. Two children can share each batch.

4. Children play with the mixture, pick it up and squeeze it. **What happens when you squeeze it? What happens when you push on it with your finger?** Try hiding a small item in the pud. Is it easy or hard to find?

why it works

This mixture acts a lot like soil or sand does when it is completely full of water. It can seem solid but then it becomes like a liquid. This is why people don't build buildings where soil is very wet—the buildings would fall down!

Prayer and Praise

What are some words to describe this mixture? (Hard. Soft. Drippy. Wet.) **God made our world in ways that show His great power.** Demonstrate an action that expresses power. **Let's thank God for His power as we make this motion each time we hear the word "power."** (Optional: Children draw pictures of powerful things in nature and then dictate prayers of thanks.)

DAY THREE: Dry Ground and Plants

Volcano!

For every four children, gather

- Small bag of potting soil (can be reused)
- 1 half-liter bottle
- Large, shallow cardboard box
- Funnel
- 1 tablespoon baking soda
- 1 tablespoon liquid dish soap
- Red food coloring
- 1 cup vinegar
- Optional—lava rock

introduce

Earth's crust is very thin compared to the rest of the layers in our planet. In some places, the crust is thin enough that when enough pressure builds up beneath it, it explodes. Let's see how that works.

Do

1. Set the bottle (with cap on loosely) in the center of your box.

2. Pour potting soil over bottle. Pat soil into a mound.

3. Open the bottle cap. Use the funnel to pour baking soda into bottle.

4. Drop a little red food coloring and the dish soap into the vinegar.

5. Pour the vinegar through the funnel into the bottle. **What happens? Why?**

why it works

The vinegar and baking soda react to create a gas (carbon dioxide). The gas builds up so much pressure that the liquid is forced out the top of the bottle as foam. When a real volcano erupts, built-up gases deep under Earth's surface push magma (melted rock) to the top. The gases and magma are called lava. When they cool, lava rock is formed. (Optional: Show a lava rock.)

Prayer and Praise

Lava rock is full of little holes where gas bubbles were mixed with magma. God gave our planet a super-heated core. Why do you think He made it that way? Students guess. **Let's thank God for our amazing planet!** Volunteers who pray pass a lava rock from one volunteer to the next. (Optional: Supply reference pictures for students to use in drawing a mural to represent a cross-section of Earth, adding a written prayer.)

DAY THREE: Dry Ground and Plants

Hot Spot Pop!

For every four children, gather

- Clear jar
- Vegetable oil
- Salt
- Water

introduce

Earth's crust is very thin compared to the core of the planet. In many places under the oceans where the crust has gotten very thin, there are what scientists call "hot spots." Let's see what underwater hot spots are like.

Do

1. Pour about ¼ inch (1.25 cm) of oil into the bottom of the jar.

2. Pour salt over the oil. Try to cover the oil with a layer of salt about ¼ inch (.6 cm) thick.

3. Fill the jar at least half full with water, tilting the jar so that the water streams down the inside of the jar and doesn't disturb the salt layer.

4. Watch and wait a minute or two. **What is happening? Why do you think these blobs are rising?**

why it works

Hot spots are places where the magma, or molten rock, is so close to the surface that it seeps out, or percolates, through the crust. In our experiment, oil (which normally floats above water) percolated up through the salt layer that had kept it underneath for a little while. The oil blobs that erupted through the salt move a lot like the blobs of magma that percolate through Earth's crust.

Prayer and Praise

Either by percolating or by a volcano, cooled magma builds up underwater as lava rock. If it builds up above the surface of the ocean, what do you think we call that? (An island.) What well-known islands are made from lava rock? (Hawaiian Islands.) **Let's thank God for the islands He has made.** (Optional: Students make islands out of flour-and-salt dough.)

DAY THREE: Dry Ground and Plants

Revealing Messages

For every four children, gather

- Shallow container of lemon juice
- Iron, heated to high heat, set on a padded surface
- 4 to 6 cotton swabs
- 8 to 12 sheets of paper
- Paper towels
- Optional—vinegar, diluted clear soda or milk

Introduce

What are some ways to send a secret message? Let's use plant power to write in invisible ink. Then we'll reveal our messages!

Do

1. Dip the swab into the lemon juice.

2. Write words or draw a picture on a sheet of paper.

3. When liquid dries, lay paper under a paper towel on the padded surface.

4. For about 20 seconds, move the iron over the paper towel to heat the paper beneath it. Remove the paper towel. (Caution: Paper will be hot.) **What do you see? Why?**

5. Optional: Use a different liquid such as soda or milk. **Does the reaction look the same? Does it seem to work in the same way?**

paper towel

message

padded surface

Why it works

As the paper gets warm, the parts of the paper that absorbed the liquid combine chemically with oxygen in the air. This is called oxidation. It makes the organic substance on the paper turn brown. It's the same thing that happens when you cut an apple and the surface turns brown, or oxidizes.

Prayer and Praise

What other fruits oxidize when they are cut? (Bananas. Pears.) **Let's name as many fruits as we can.** Invite volunteers to thank God for fruit, naming fruits mentioned by others. (Optional: Students use materials from experiments to write or draw a prayer to God. Invite them to take paper home to heat later.)

DAY THREE: Dry Ground and Plants

Enzymes in Action

For every child, gather

- Slice of raw potato

- Small cup filled halfway with hydrogen peroxide

- Optional—pieces of other raw vegetables and more hydrogen peroxide

Introduce

Enzymes are proteins that cause chemical reactions to happen. Living things—plants, insects, animals and all living things—contain enzymes. Let's see if we can prove that potatoes contain enzymes!

Do

1. Sniff the liquid in your cup. Is it water? (It is hydrogen peroxide. We sometimes use it to clean cuts.)

2. Drop your potato slice into the cup. **What do you see happening? What do you think is causing the bubbles?**

3. Optional: Test other raw foods with fresh hydrogen peroxide.

Why it works

The potato contains an enzyme called catalase. The enzyme is actually changing the hydrogen peroxide into water and oxygen bubbles! Enzymes are not changed when they make these reactions happen. They can be used again and again.

Prayer and Praise

God put enzymes into every plant and every other living thing. Scientists have counted about 5,000 different ones so far! God made every detail of His creation to work together. Let's work together to thank Him. Invite students to divide into two groups: First group names something living that God made and the second group responds with another living thing God made whose name begins with the same first letter (apples and anchovies, bananas and butter, etc.). Volunteers take turns from each group to pray sentence prayers of thanks to God.

DAY THREE: Dry Ground and Plants

A tiny Ecosystem

For every four children, gather

- 4 clear containers with lids or stoppers (canning jars, plastic 2-liter bottles with caps, etc.)
- Potting soil
- Gravel
- Funnels
- Long handled spoons, chopsticks or tongs
- Small plants, rocks, etc. (can collect these on a nature walk)
- Water in a pitcher

Introduce

What do plants need to live? (Water. Sunlight. Soil.) **Today we are going to create tiny ecosystems. They will show us how plants, soil, sunlight and water work together.**

Do

1. Drop a layer of gravel in the bottom of your jar about 1 inch (2.5 cm) deep. Use a funnel if needed.

2. Add a layer of potting soil about 2 inches (5 cm) deep.

3. Use a chopstick or spoon to make a hole in the soil. Plant at least one plant. Pour a little water into the soil around your plant.

4. Add stones, shells or other items if you wish. Now close the top tightly.

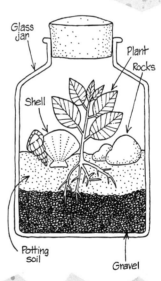

Glass Jar, Plant, Rocks, Shell, Potting soil, Gravel

Why it works

Take your ecosystem home and set it near a sunny window. You won't need to add more water for about a month. Look at it every day to see how the plant grows and how the water moves from the soil to the top. On Earth, water is drawn by sunlight from soil and into the clouds.

Prayer and Praise

God created the water and plants and sun to work together to make what we call the water cycle. If there were no rain, what would happen? (Nothing would grow. We would starve.) **Let's each thank God for a different food that comes from a plant.** Students pray sentence prayers. (Optional: Students draw a mural of a garden on large butcher paper, adding written prayers.)

Solid Vibrations

For every child, gather

- 2-foot (61-cm) length of string
- Piece of masking tape

Introduce

In an earthquake, waves or vibrations move through the ground from the earthquake site. Imagine you are a scientist. How could you tell what materials these waves move through? Here's a simple test.

Do

1. Tape one end of your string down to the table.

2. Stretch the string. Pluck it so it vibrates. Notice the sound.

3. Now wrap the string around your finger several times.

4. Put the tip of your "string finger" in your ear. Pluck the string again. **What do you notice? Why do you think this is so?**

a.

b.

why it works

The sound of the vibrating string is louder when your finger is in your ear. But that isn't only because the string is closer. It's because the string is attached to something solid (your head). The vibrations move faster through the bones in your head! In the same way, earthquake waves move more quickly through dense materials (like rock). This gives scientists clues about the density of the materials through which those waves traveled.

Prayer and Praise

Even with things we cannot see, God made His world perfectly. What are some of the perfect ways in which God made the world? Students give ideas. God made His world so that we can trust the way things work in the world He made. Let's thank God for making the world just right! (Optional: Students draw and write prayers of thanks to God for making the world perfect.)

DAY THREE: Dry Ground and Plants

Helicopter Seeds

For every four children, gather

- 4 strips of paper about ¾x6 inches (1.9x15 cm)
- 4 paper clips
- Ruler
- Pencil
- Scissors

introduce

God made many different kinds of seeds so that plants can reproduce, or make more plants. Different seeds move in different ways. Today we'll see how one kind of seed moves!

Do

1. Measure and draw a line 2 inches (5 cm) long down the center of the strip.

2. Cut a slit along the line, folding each resulting piece in an opposite direction.

3. Fold in the corners of the uncut end. Attach the paper clip to this end.

4. Toss your helicopter seed model into the air to see how it flies!

a. b. c. 2 in (5 cm) d.

why it works

God made the seeds of maple trees (and some other trees) so that they move like our paper helicopters do. The seed is at the bottom (like the paper clip). When the seed falls from the tree, instead of falling straight down, it spins like a helicopter so that the seed moves away from the tree to where there will be more space for it to grow.

Prayer and Praise

What are some other ways God made for seeds to move? (Stick to whatever passes by. Pop. Fall. Blow in the wind.) Why do you think God made so many ways for seeds to move? Let's thank God for the variety of seeds He made! (Optional: Students draw and show pictures of other kinds of seeds and how they move.)

DAY THREE: Dry Ground and Plants

Vegetable People

For every four children, gather

- 3 to 5 kinds of vegetables (carrots, broccoli, celery, peppers, squash, etc.) cut into strips and chunks ahead of time
- Toothpicks in a container
- Paper plates and napkins
- Vegetable dip (such as Ranch dressing) in a container

Introduce

One of the wonderful things about the third day of creation is that God made things for us to EAT! What vegetables do you see here? Today's challenge is to create an edible vegetable person from these cut-up vegetables.

Do

1. *Teacher: Ahead of time, post a note alerting parents to the use of food in this activity. Also check registration forms for possible food allergies.*
2. Take a paper plate to work on. Choose cut-up vegetable pieces.
3. Attach pieces together with toothpicks to make a person (or animal or sculpture—you may want to make more than one!).
4. Grab a napkin and some veggie dip. Enjoy!

Why it works

God made many more kinds of vegetables than most of us have ever eaten. Because they are plants that absorb sunlight and the minerals from the soil and water, they are a very important source of vitamins and minerals. What are some vegetables you eat often? Some you've never eaten?

Prayer and Praise

Why do you think God made so many kinds of vegetables? Think of your favorite vegetable. Let's take turns to thank God for each of those kinds of vegetables! Students pray sentence prayers. (Optional: Students draw pictures of favorite vegetables on large butcher paper, adding written prayers.)

DAY THREE: Dry Ground and Plants

Nature Press

For every child, gather

- Two 6x8-inch (15x20.5-cm) rectangles of corrugated cardboard
- 6x17-inch (15x43-cm) rectangle of poster board
- Markers, glue, nature pictures, etc., for decoration
- Rubber bands
- A plant identification book for your area

introduce

One way to study plants is to save samples of them. An easy way to do this is by using a nature press. Let's each make a press so that we can keep samples of plants we want to identify.

Do

1. Fold the poster board in half to make a book shape. Write your name and "My Nature Press" on the front of the poster board book.

2. Decorate book with pictures or drawings.

3. Glue one corrugated cardboard rectangle onto each inner side of the poster board book, leaving 1 inch (2.5 cm) of space in the center.

4. Secure the press with at least two rubber bands. Once the glue is dry, you are ready to take plant samples and press them for future study!

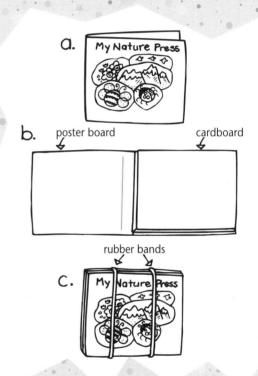

a. My Nature Press

b. poster board   cardboard

rubber bands

c. My Nature Press

why it works

Because the corrugated cardboard has tunnels inside it, air passes freely through the middle of it. This makes drying a plant sample easier. When plant samples are pressed tightly by the rubber bands, they stay in their original shapes so that we can study them.

Prayer and Praise

Show a plant identification book. People who have studied plants that grow where we live have taken pictures and identified the plants that grow wild here. God has made many more kinds of plants than are in any book! How many kinds of flowers do you think we can name? Students name flowers. Invite volunteers to then thank God for one or more of the kinds of flowers mentioned. (Optional: Students write prayers and place them inside their nature presses to take home and read later.)

DAY THREE: Dry Ground and Plants

Soil Shakers

For every four children, gather

- Loaf pan
- Sand to fill pan to half its depth
- Water
- Thin brick
- Rubber mallet or stick

introduce

God made water and land. But there are times when people fill, or dump soil, to make more land at the edge of water. Let's see what earthquakes do to filled land.

Do

1. Fill pan halfway with sand.

2. Pour enough water into the pan to fill it to just below the sand's surface.

3. Push the narrow end of the brick far enough into the wet sand so that it stands like a tall building.

4. Tap the side of the pan with a mallet or stick repeatedly. **What happens?**

why it works

When soil (or sand) is added at the water's edge, water flows into the tiny spaces between the grains. The soil looks and acts like a solid, but when an earthquake (tapping the pan) suddenly squeezes soil particles together, the water molecules are trapped. They can't flow away, so the water pressure increases. For just a moment, the water pressure forces the sand particles apart from each other! This is called liquefaction. A building (the brick) falls when the grains of sand are not touching. Plop!

Prayer and Praise

Let's list some places God has made for people to live. (Islands. Land. Water. Jungles.) Invite volunteers to choose one place to live for which they thank God in a sentence prayer. (Optional: Students write and draw list on butcher paper.)

DAY THREE: Dry Ground and Plants

cabbage: the Acid test

For every four children, gather

- Red cabbage in a medium-sized bowl (can be grated ahead of time)
- Thermal carafe of hot water
- Strainer or colander
- Plastic pitcher
- Several clear plastic cups
- Liquids to test (lemon juice, vinegar, soft drink, etc.)
- Baking soda and teaspoon

introduce

Chemists test substances in many ways to learn more about them. Today we're going be chemists. We'll use red cabbage to test whether or not a substance is an acid (something sour).

Do

1. Tear (or grate) cabbage into tiny pieces.

2. Cover cabbage with hot water. Let it sit (10-15 minutes) until water is purple.

3. Strain cabbage water into a plastic pitcher and then pour a small amount of cabbage juice into each plastic cup.

4. Test a liquid: Pour a small amount of liquid into one cup. **Is the cabbage water turning pinkish?** Try another liquid to see what color it turns. Now add baking soda to one cup of cabbage water. **What happens?**

why it works

The red cabbage water is called an indicator. It contains chemicals that react in the presence of acids and bases. The cabbage water turns pink or reddish when mixed with acids and bluish when mixed with bases (substances that are not acids).

Prayer and Praise

Let's name other plants God made. What do we use those plants for besides eating? (Clothing. Oxygen. Fuel. Building. Shade.) Ask several questions that can be answered, "Because God made plants!" Encourage students to repeat the phrase with you. Then pray together, inviting students to thank God for plants He made.

DAY THREE: Dry Ground and Plants

Food Factories

For every four children, gather

- 4 wooden blocks or hammers
- Green leaves, flowers and stems from a variety of green plants
- Sections of old white bedsheets
- Newspaper

introduce

How do plants make food? Today we're going to explore the food factories of plants—in a really fun way!

Do

1. Lay a section of newspaper in front of you.

2. Lay a section of sheet on the newspaper and lay some plant parts on the sheet.

3. Lay another piece of sheet over the plant parts and newspaper over that.

4. Pound with the block or hammer until everything is very flat. Lift off the top newspaper and sheet. Peel off the bits of plant matter. **What is left? What do you see? Try it again!**

News-paper

Sheet

why it works

The green substance left on your cloth is called chlorophyll. Chlorophyll makes plants green. But it also has a very important job within the plant. Chlorophyll captures the sun's energy and converts it into food for the plant by combining it with carbon dioxide, water and minerals that have been taken up through the roots.

Prayer and Praise

What green things do you eat every day? We don't always think about how hamburger came from green plants. But what did the cow eat? Students think of other examples of foods that come from green plants. Invite a volunteer from each group to thank God, pausing for others in their group to include plants they mentioned. (Optional: Students draw a mural of foods and illustrate how those foods came from green plants, adding written prayers of thanks to God.)

DAY THREE: Dry Ground and Plants

Lemons: Plant Power!

For every four children, gather

- 2 lemons, slit as shown
- 3 coated copper wires with bare ends, each about 18 inches (45.5 cm) long
- 2 large steel paper clips
- 2 shiny copper pennies
- Battery-powered digital clock
- Scissors

introduce

How many things do you own that use batteries? Today we'll find out how God made some plants that can be used like batteries!

Do

1. Attach one paperclip to the end of one wire.

2. Wind the end of another wire around a penny.

3. Attach the second penny to one end of the third wire and a paperclip to its other end.

4. Roll the lemons on the table to loosen their pulp.

5. Find the two small slits in the skin of each lemon.

6. Slide the paper clip attached to the wire and the penny through a slit.

7. Slide the penny into a slit in the other lemon.

8. Put the other paper clip into the second slit of the lemon with the penny.

9. Slide the last penny into the last open slit.

10. Connect the two free ends of the wires to the battery terminals of the digital clock. If you've hooked everything up and the clock does not run, switch the wires.

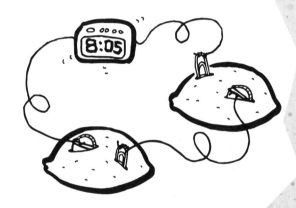

why it works

The steel in the paper clip makes a chemical reaction with the lemon juice. The copper in the penny makes a different reaction. These two different chemical reactions push electrons through the wires harder in one direction than the other so that the electrons flow. If the reactions were not different, no electrons would be pushed. As the electrons flow, they power the clock. That's electrical current!

Prayer and Praise

How do you think people got the idea for batteries? Invite a volunteer to thank God for plants and for people who learn new things from plants.

DAY THREE: Dry Ground and Plants

Dirt Dust

For every two children, gather

- Sheets of newspaper spread over work surface
- Variety of softer and harder rocks (sandstone, granite, etc.)
- Protective goggles and work gloves

Introduce

What do you think soil is made from? One part of soil comes from rocks that have been ground into particles and dust over a long time by the wind, sun and rain. Let's see if we can make particles and dust from these rocks.

Do

1. Put on gloves and goggles.

2. Set two rocks on the newspaper.

3. Hit the rocks together carefully, so you don't hurt your fingers!

4. Try using other rocks. **Are they softer or harder? How can you tell?**

5. When everyone has had a turn, fold the newspapers together to gather rock bits and dust into a pile. **How is this like soil? How is it different?**

why it works

This experiment not only shows us that soil contains rock particles and dust but also that some rocks are harder than others! It takes longer for weather to wear down harder rocks into soil. The process can take thousands of years.

Prayer and Praise

The Bible says that God's love endures forever. How many thousands of years do you think that is? What else do you know about God's love? Students tell. Pray, thanking God for His love and including students' ideas. (Optional: Students use markers to write descriptive words about God on rocks.)

Leaf observation

For every child, gather

- At least 1 leaf (Leaves may be from a variety of plants. If all leaves are from the same plant, provide extra leaves to increase the challenge.)

- Paper and pencil

introduce

A basic part of being a scientist is being a careful observer. Today we're going to work on our observing skills, using these leaves. God made many kinds of leaves. And even on the same plant, every leaf is different!

Do

1. Taking a leaf from the pile, look at it very carefully. Notice its size, color, the way it feels, its shape and whatever marks or features might help you to remember your leaf.

2. Use paper and pencil to take notes or draw pictures to help you remember details about the observed leaf.

3. After at least three minutes, lay your leaf back in the pile. Mix up all the leaves. **Can you find your leaf? How can you tell?**

why it works

Observation means looking at and paying close attention to something. All other steps in the scientific process are based on good observations. Then scientists make a hypothesis (a guess based on the observation). What hypothesis about leaves could you make based on what you observed?

Prayer and Praise

What are some other things that might seem to be the same but that are different from each other? (Snowflakes. Stars.) Invite each student to insert his or her idea into your prayer as you thank God for the amazing world He made for us to observe. (Optional: Students make a mural by drawing and gluing leaves to large butcher paper and writing prayers.)

DAY FOUR

Sun, Moon and Stars

"And God said, 'Let there be lights in the expanse of the sky to separate the day from the night, and let them serve as signs to mark seasons and days and years, and let them be lights in the expanse of the sky to give light on the earth.' And it was so. God made two great lights—the greater light to govern the day and the lesser light to govern the night. He also made the stars. God set them in the expanse of the sky to give off light on the earth, to govern the day and the night, and to separate light from darkness. And God saw that it was good. And there was evening, and there was morning—the fourth day."

Genesis 1:14-19

Here are experiments to help your kids understand aspects of our solar system and some of the natural laws related to our planet!

Space Shape Match

For every four children, gather

- Variety of textured papers (sandpaper, wallpaper, shelf liner, fabric swatches, plastic wrap, bubble wrap, etc.)
- Scissors
- Large paper bag

introduce

What are the names of the lights God put in the sky? Today we're going to play a game where we match the shapes of those lights.

Do

1. Ahead of time, cut textured papers into sun, moon and star shapes, at least one match for every shape and for every texture of paper. Place one set of finished shapes in paper bag. Lay one set of shapes out on the floor.

2. Invite children to take turns to select a shape from the bag and then match it with its mate (by both shape and texture).

3. For each new round of play, vary the way children select shapes to match (lay shapes facedown in a star pattern, hide them around the room, etc.).

why it works

The sun always looks round. The moon sometimes looks round and sometimes like it is growing larger or smaller. That's the reason we cut a crescent shape for the moon. The moon is a planet. It's bumpy like some of our moon shapes. It looks like it has a face because of the shadows made by the bumps!

prayer and praise

Let's thank God for one of the lights He put in the sky. **Dear God,** (child's name) **thanks You for . . .** Children take turns to say either "sun," "moon" or "stars" as you pause during prayer. (Optional: Children draw daytime and nighttime murals and thank God for sun, moon and stars.)

Moon on the Lagoon

For every four children, gather

- Dishpan half full of water
- Sand table filled with sand
- Small toy boats and floating toys
- Eggbeaters

introduce

How do the sun and moon help us? While we play with our boats, let's pretend they are in the ocean. The moon helps ocean water move.

Do

1. Ahead of time, set the dishpan of water into a hole in the center of the sand table so that top edge is even with the sand level. Place small boats and floating toys on the sand.

2. Children explore the lagoon in the sand table by using toys on the water and in the sand. Invite children to blow on the water to observe the reactions of toy boats.

3. Children use eggbeaters to create waves in the water. Tip the dishpan to flow water up onto the sand to give an example of what it is like when the tide rises.

why it works

When we watch the ocean, we can see that the water is sometimes close to us and sometimes far away. The moon and the sun make that happen.

Prayer and Praise

God made the moon and sun to do more than give light. They also help to control the water that moves in the oceans. Let's thank God for His great power. He loves us very much! Invite children to repeat after you, phrase by phrase: **Dear God, thank You for making the sun and moon. Thank You for making the ocean. You are great. In Jesus' name, amen.** (Optional: Children watercolor a wave mural on large butcher paper. Write a prayer on the mural.)

Solar wind

For every four children, gather

- Towels
- Dishpan or baking dish
- Pitcher of water
- Styrofoam peanuts

introduce

On Earth, what are some things we see when the wind blows? On the sun, there is a kind of wind, too. It is called solar wind.

Do

1. Ahead of time, cover work area with towels and set dishpan or baking dish on towels.

2. Children pour water into the bottom of the dish and blow on the water to make ripples on the surface. **What is happening to the water? What happens if you blow harder?**

3. Children place Styrofoam peanuts in the water and then blow them back and forth across the surface of the water. **How else could you make wind that can move the Styrofoam peanut?**

why it works

We made a little wind by blowing air. Our moving air moved the water and the Styrofoam peanut. On the sun, the solar wind is a very fast and strong wind. It is made by the hot, burning gases of the sun.

Prayer and Praise

What do we call it when we can see the sun in the sky? Think of something you like to do in the daytime. When I say your name, you can tell us what you like to do. Pray, **Dear God, (Jena) likes to** (child responds) **in the daytime.** Repeat for each child and then say, **Thank You, God, for the daytime. In Jesus' name, amen.** (Optional: Children work together to glue torn yellow, orange and red paper to make a large sun mosaic on butcher paper, dictating words for a written prayer.)

DAY FOUR: Sun, Moon and Stars

Stand and jump

For every four children, gather

- Yarn
- Masking tape
- Markers
- Measuring stick

introduce

Let's see how far we can jump today. Then we'll see how far we could jump if we were on the moon!

Do

1. Make a yarn line on the floor.

2. Children take turns standing at the yarn line and jumping as far as possible with both feet together. Mark the distance with a masking-tape piece lettered with each child's name or initials.

3. Assist children in using measuring sticks to measure the length of their jumps. Then choose one child's distance and multiply the number by six. Measure that distance out slowly. Mark the final distance with a piece of masking tape. (Repeat with other children's distances as time and interest allow.)

why it works

The distance I marked is a long way farther than (Spencer) jumped! But on the moon, you could jump about six times as far as you can on Earth. That's because gravity is not as strong on the moon as it is on Earth. Gravity is what pulls us down toward the ground.

Prayer and Praise

If God had not made gravity, we would float up into the sky! I'm glad God always cares for us! That's one reason to thank Him. What is one way we could show our thanks to God for all the ways He helps us? Children respond. Pray, sing or thank God in whatever way the children chose. (Optional: Children draw self-portraits. Add each child's dictated "thank You" prayer to his or her drawing.)

DAY FOUR: Sun, Moon and Stars

Heavy or Light?

For every four children, gather

- 1 or more household or bathroom scales
- Items to weigh (blocks, balls, toys, etc.)

introduce

Hold up two items. **Which of these things do you think is heavier?** On the moon, things don't weigh as much as they do here. Today we're going to think about how heavy or light things are.

Do

1. Children take turns carrying an item around the room and then weighing item on scales. (If you have provided bathroom scales, children may wish to weigh themselves.)

2. To increase the challenge, help children compare the items. **Which item is the heaviest? Which of these two items is the lightest? Which item would be hard to carry for a long time?**

3. Weigh a fairly heavy item and note its weight. Then divide that number by six. See if you can find something that weighs about that amount for comparison.

why it works

When we weighed the (truck), it weighed six pounds. But on the moon, this truck would only weigh as much as this block. It weighs one pound. Gravity is not as strong on the moon as it is on Earth. Children take turns to hold both items to compare the weight difference.

Prayer and Praise

If we were on the moon, would God be with us? Yes! The Bible says God is always with us and will watch over us. He loves us. Let's thank Him for being with us. Children take turns to pray a sentence prayer: **Thank You, God, that You are always with me.** (Optional: Children use sponges to paint moon shapes. Add a written prayer and read it aloud.)

DAY FOUR: Sun, Moon and Stars

Kitchen Space Science

For every four children, gather

- Newspaper to cover surfaces
- 4 clear plastic cups
- Measuring cups and spoons
- Small bottles of vinegar
- Baking soda in open containers

introduce

The sun, moon and stars are out in space. Everywhere in space, there are gases. Let's do an experiment to make gases here on Earth!

Do

1. Distribute clear cups. With adult help, children pour ¼ cup vinegar into their cups, add 1 teaspoon of baking soda and then observe the reaction.

2. Repeat this activity as time and interest allow. Children will want to try it several times!

why it works

When some things are mixed together, something happens that is called a reaction. This reaction makes a gas. That's what causes the bubbles. In space, there are many gases. Some of the gases are burning. The sun is a ball of burning gases.

Prayer and Praise

What shines at night besides the moon? (Stars.) The stars are also made of burning gases. God put the stars in the sky. We see the stars at night. What are things you do at night? Children respond. Thank God for nighttime, including children's responses as you pray. (Optional: Children draw a nighttime mural, dictating prayers of thanks to be written on mural.)

Balloon Blow-up

For every four children, gather

- Paper plate
- 2 envelopes of baker's yeast
- 2 magnifying glasses
- Narrow-necked bottle (ketchup, etc.) with lid
- Sugar
- Very warm (not hot) water
- Balloon
- Shallow pan

introduce

The air we breathe is made up of gases. We usually blow up a balloon by blowing into it. But let's see if we can make it bigger by making some gases!

Do

1. Ahead of time, pour an envelope of yeast onto a paper plate so children can examine it with magnifying glasses. Pour other envelope of yeast into the bottle.

2. With adult help, children add sugar and warm water to bottle according to package directions.

3. Screw lid on bottle. Invite children to take turns shaking bottle to mix ingredients.

4. When ingredients are mixed, remove lid. An adult stretches the neck of the balloon over the neck of the bottle.

5. Pour rest of warm water in a shallow pan. Set bottle in pan.

6. Watch to see the balloon inflate. **What makes this happen?**

Yeast Sugar Warm water

why it works

Yeast is a tiny plant. When we add warm water and sugar, the plant begins to grow. As it grows, this plant gives off a gas. That gas filled the bottle and then moved up into the balloon so that it made the balloon bigger!

Prayer and Praise

There are many gases in space. Some gases burn to make the stars shine. We call the gases around our planet "air." Let's thank God for the air we breathe. Let's say this poem together: "Thank You, God, for good fresh air. It's around us everywhere!" Repeat the poem several times with children and close by saying, **In Jesus' name, amen.**

Tadpole Race

For every four children, gather

- 2 jars of water
- Yellow and blue food coloring
- Cardboard covered with waxed paper (secure with masking tape)
- Chair or blocks
- Eyedroppers

Introduce

Gravity is what keeps us all on the ground instead of floating off into space. Gravity can also make things move faster. Let's see how that works.

Do

1. Add yellow food coloring to one jar of water and blue to the other.

2. Use a chair or blocks under one end of cardboard to make a ramp.

3. Children take turns to squeeze out a drop of yellow water at the top of the ramp while other children squeeze a drop of blue beside it. **Does one drop go faster than the other? What happens if you raise the end of the ramp to make it steeper?**

4. Try placing drops very close to each other. As drops race downward together, they will merge together to form a green drop. It looks like a little tadpole racing down the incline!

Why it works

When we make the ramp steeper, the drops move faster. When the ramp is flatter, the drops don't move as fast. Gravity pulls the drops faster when the incline is steeper.

Prayer and Praise

God made gravity so that we would not have to worry about flying away into space. **Let's thank Him.** Invite children to jump up one at a time and say, **Thank You, God, for gravity!** (Optional: Children draw pictures of experiment and dictate prayers to add to pictures.)

DAY FOUR: Sun, Moon and Stars

Starry Art

For every four children, gather

- 4 to 8 sheets of black construction paper
- Crayons
- ½ cup warm water into which ½ cup Epsom Salts is dissolved
- Paintbrushes

Introduce

What do you think it looks like out in space? Today we'll draw space pictures. Then we will do something special to make stars appear in our pictures!

Do

1. Children draw space pictures. **Be sure to include planets and rockets!**

2. When pictures are finished, children paint over pictures with the warm water mixture.

3. When papers have dried, invite children to look at their space pictures. **What do you see? Where do you think the crystal stars came from?**

Epsom Salts Solution

Why it works

The water we painted over our pictures contained a kind of salt. The salt in the water formed crystals on our papers as it dried out (evaporated). The crystals look like stars!

Prayer and Praise

God made the stars to shine in the sky. When we can see the stars, we know it is nighttime. What is something you like to do at night? Children respond. Let's thank God for making the stars! We'll make our fingers move like little stars as we pray. Demonstrate opening and closing fingers to look like the rays of a star. (Optional: Children dictate prayers to an adult, who adds prayers to space pictures.)

DAY FOUR: Sun, Moon and Stars

Magnetic Fields

For every four children, gather

- 4 to 8 small magnets (bar magnets will best show north and south poles)
- 4 sheets of paper
- Iron filings (available from school-supply or scientific-supply stores)

Introduce

What's the biggest thing you have ever seen a magnet lift? Let's explore some magnets to learn more about magnetic fields. Did you know there is a magnetic field on the sun, too?

Do

1. Lay one or two magnets on a table.

2. Lay a sheet of paper over the magnets.

3. Scatter some iron filings over the paper. **What happens?**

4. Try this with different magnets. **Is the pattern always the same?**

Why it works

The pattern made by the iron filings looks a lot like the pattern of Earth's magnetic fields. Earth's magnetic fields are force fields that extend far out into space. These fields are fairly stable. That means they don't change very much. The sun has magnetic fields, too. But the sun's magnetic fields are different. They go through a cycle of change about every 11 years! Sunspots and solar winds are two of the results of these changes in the sun's magnetic fields.

Prayer and Praise

Scientists don't understand why and how the magnetic fields change on the sun. But they do know that part of the job of Earth's magnetic field is to protect us from dangerous solar radiation. God protects us in ways we can't even see! **What are other ways God protects us?** Invite students to create a motion for the word "protection." **Let's thank God for His protection that shows us He loves and cares for us.** Students use the motion they created whenever the word "protection" is spoken during prayer time. (Optional: Students draw and write on large butcher paper to make a mural about God's protection.)

DAY FOUR: Sun, Moon and Stars

itty-Bitty Electromagnet

For every two children, gather

- C- or D-cell battery
- 2 feet (.6 m) of insulated bell wire (with 1 inch [2.5 cm] of insulation removed from either end)
- 3-inch (7.5-cm) nail
- Electrical tape
- Paper clips

introduce

Magnetic fields occur naturally on the sun and on Earth. But can we create magnets by using electricity? Let's see!

Do

1. Grab the wire in the middle. Wrap it around the nail, leaving a few inches of loose wire on either end. Leave about 1 inch (2.5 cm) of the nail point exposed. (Children ask for adult help as needed.)

2. Tape the point end of the wire to the bottom of the battery.

3. Set the battery on a table. Place paper clips nearby.

4. Holding the unconnected wire by its plastic covering, touch the exposed wire to the top of the battery. **What happens?** Try again.

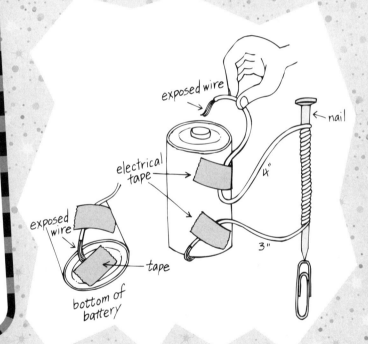

exposed wire

electrical tape

exposed wire

tape

bottom of battery

nail

4"

3"

why it works

When the wire touches the positive charge of the battery, the electricity stored inside the battery flows through the wire to create a magnetic field. It magnetizes the nail. When you break the electrical circuit, the nail loses its magnetic pull. (If a nail stays magnetized, hit it on the table to demagnetize.)

Prayer and Praise

Magnetism is a law God made at creation. What are other natural laws? (Gravity. Inertia.) God made laws by which everything acts. He gave us laws by which to act, too. Both kinds of laws help us to trust that things (and people) will act in predictable ways! Let's thank God for this way He shows His love for us. Volunteers thank God for His laws and include their ideas.

DAY FOUR: Sun, Moon and Stars

Moon Face

For every four children, gather

- Flashlight
- 6 to 8 dominoes

introduce

When you see the full moon, what do you think it looks like? Today we'll find out why the moon looks the way it does!

Do

1. Set up the dominoes in any way you like.

2. Darken the room and shine the flashlight at the dominoes from about 12 inches (30.5 cm) away. Don't look at the dominoes but at the pattern of shadows.

3. Change the angle of the flashlight to see how the shadows change.

4. Move the dominoes into a different pattern to see if you can make a pattern of shadows that look like the face of "the man in the moon."

why it works

The moon is not a smooth planet. It has mountain areas, or highlands. They reflect brightly, like a white wall. It also has flat areas (called maria), which don't reflect as well. The insides of craters also are shadowed. The patterns of light and shadow we call "the man in the moon" are called "the rabbit" by Native Americans. Next time you look at a full moon, see if you can find the rabbit shape—or another shape!

Prayer and Praise

When we see the things God made, we each might notice something different about them. What is something else you have noticed about the moon? (Gets larger and smaller. Influences tides.) God made us able to notice different things so that we can learn from each other. Let's put each group's dominoes together so we have enough to lay out the words "thank you" to God. (Optional: If time permits, try arranging dominoes and using a flashlight to make the domino shadows spell out "thank you.")

DAY FOUR: Sun, Moon and Stars

The Blue Planet

For every four children, gather

- Clear glass or jar filled with water
- Flashlight
- Eyedropper
- Milk in open container
- Spoon

Introduce

When we see pictures of Earth from outer space, what color does it look like? (Blue.) **Let's find out the reason!**

Do

1. Darken the room and shine the flashlight through the glass of water. Look through the side of the glass to notice how the water looks with the light shining through it.

2. Add several drops of milk to the water and stir.

3. Now shine the flashlight through the glass again. Look through the side of the glass again. **How does the water look different? Add more milk. How does adding more milk change the color?**

Why it works

Milk particles in the clear water scatter the shorter blue light waves and make the water look bluish. In the same way, air and water molecules in our atmosphere scatter the shorter blue waves in sunlight. This is what makes the sky look blue from Earth's surface. It also makes the planet look blue from outer space. When light shines through clean, dry air, we see the bluest sky. At sunset, when the sunlight is coming from the horizon, it has to travel through a lot more particles. The shorter blue waves are scattered before they reach our eyes, but the longer red and orange waves still get through. That is why the sunset is reddish-orange.

Prayer and Praise

From outer space, our planet looks blue. What planet looks red from space? (Mars.) Let's each choose a color. In 10 seconds, see how many things you can name that are that color! Students take turns to name a color and items of that color. Volunteers thank God for something He created in the color they chose. (Optional: Students draw a mural of outer space, adding written prayers.)

Eclipse

For every four children, gather

- Bible
- Basketball
- Tennis ball or softball
- Flashlight

introduce

When have you seen an eclipse? What do you think causes an eclipse? Today we're going to create small eclipses to help us understand how they work.

Do

1. To represent Earth, set the basketball on a table. Ask a teammate to hold it steady.

2. To represent the moon, ask another teammate to hold out the tennis ball with two fingers, away from his or her body.

3. Ask another teammate to turn off the lights.

4. Stand on the far side of the room, pointing the flashlight at both the tennis ball and the basketball.

5. To represent the sun, turn on the flashlight. **What do you see?** This is like what happens during a solar eclipse.

6. If you move the tennis ball around the basketball until it's on the dark side, you'll see what looks like a lunar eclipse!

why it works

In a solar eclipse, a shadow cast by the moon shows on the Earth. During a lunar eclipse, the shadow that falls across the moon is from Earth.

Prayer and Praise

The way our solar system works is amazing! Invite a student to read Psalm 8:1-4. It sounds like King David was amazed at the way God made our solar system, too! Let's repeat the first verse of this psalm as a prayer. Repeat several times.

DAY FOUR: Sun, Moon and Stars

twinkle, twinkle

For every four children, gather

- Bible
- Shoebox
- Nail
- Index card
- Pushpin
- Tape
- Short piece of thread
- Lamp

introduce

What are some words people use to describe stars? Have you ever wondered why stars seem to twinkle? Here's an experiment to help us find out!

Do

1. Punch three nail holes in one end of the box.

2. Punch one nail hole in the other end for a viewer.

3. With the pushpin, punch at least 25 holes in the index card.

4. Tape both ends of a short piece of thread to the top of the card and then tape the thread loop to the inside of the shoebox lid about 2 inches (5 cm) from the end with three holes. Put the lid on the box.

5. As you gently rock the box back and forth, look through the viewer toward the lamp. **What do you see?**

why it works

The holes in one end of the box are like stars. In space, there is nothing to stop their rays. But when you see the lights through the viewer, they twinkle. That's because the card with the holes acts like the Earth's atmosphere. It lets only part of the light through. When starlight reaches Earth's atmosphere, air movement scatters and deflects the starlight. It makes the stars seem to twinkle.

Prayer and Praise

Read Psalm 147:4 aloud. With all the billions of stars in the universe, God calls each one by name! He knows your name, too, even though there are billions of people. When might a kid your age feel like he or she doesn't matter? Students respond. You matter to God. He made you and knows all about you. Pray, **Dear God, thank You that you know** (each student says own name aloud) **by name.** (Optional: Students draw starry sky pictures, adding the words of Psalm 147:4 to their drawings.)

DAY FOUR: Sun, Moon and Stars

Always Shining

For every four children, gather

- 4 index cards
- Hole punches
- 4 white envelopes
- Flashlight

introduce

We have all seen stars shine at night. But what happens to the stars during the day? This experiment will help us see whether they shine or not!

Do

1. Randomly punch 10 to 20 holes in your index card.

2. Slide the punched card into the envelope.

3. Hold the envelope in front of you. Shine the flashlight on the front of the envelope from about 2 inches (5 cm) away. **Do you see the holes in the card?**

4. Now move the flashlight behind the envelope. Shine the flashlight on the back of the envelope from about 2 inches (5 cm) away. **What do you see?**

why it works

The holes in the card can't be seen when you shine light on the front. But when you shine it on the back, they are easily seen. The light in the room always passes through the holes in the card, but only when the light from the flashlight is brighter than the room's light can you see the holes. In the same way, the stars shine all the time, but sunlight is so bright that starlight is not seen. But when the sky is dark, stars are very visible!

Prayer and Praise

God created many stars. What constellations can we name? (Big Dipper. Pleiades.) Let's thank God for the stars we see. Students who named constellations include those names in sentence prayers. (Optional: Students write and draw prayers of thanks, drawing "constellations" that spell out words.)

to the Moon!

For every four children, gather

- 4 balloons
- Marker
- 4 small binder clips
- 4 drinking straws
- Masking tape
- 14-foot (4.2-m) length of string

introduce

What do you think people had to know to travel to the moon? One natural law they used is that for every action, there is an equal and opposite reaction. That is the first law of motion. Let's do an experiment that shows the laws of motion.

Do

1. Blow up your balloon. Write your name on it.

2. Let it go. **Does it go across the room? What happens?**

3. Blow up your balloon again. Clip it closed.

4. Tape a straw along the side of the balloon.

5. Thread an end of the string through the straw.

6. Hold your end and have a partner hold the other end of the string taut.

7. Release the binder clip. **What happens?**

8. Try each balloon. Compare results.

straw

14-foot string

binder clip

balloon

why it works

At first, the balloons moved in the opposite direction of the air escaping from inside them. Jets and rockets move in the same way. But by adding the straw and the string, we created a guidance system that allows the same amount of thrust to push the balloon more efficiently to its target. To get to the moon, a rocket needs both enough thrust to get outside Earth's orbit and then a way to direct it into the moon's orbit.

Prayer and Praise

God made the universe so that the laws of motion work together. What are other things in nature that work together? (Rain and sun. Heat and cooling.) **Let's thank God for His great wisdom.** Volunteers pray, thanking God for the way nature works together and repeating other students' ideas. (Optional: Students read and illustrate Psalm 19:1-4 on a mural.)

orbiter

For every child, gather

- Deli or yogurt container
- Hole punch (to share)
- 4 lengths of string: 3 about 10 inches (25.5 cm) long, 1 about 3 feet (.9 m) long
- Lightweight item to place in the container (table tennis ball, etc.)
- Optional—water in a pitcher

introduce

Did you ever wonder why the moon and planets orbit in a circle? Here is a fun way to understand centripetal force!

Do

1. Punch three holes equal distances apart near the top of your container.

2. Tie one end of each short string securely through each hole.

3. Tie the loose string ends together, and then tie the long string to their knot.

4. Place an item in the container. Hold the long string TIGHTLY and begin to spin the container at an angle. **Does the item fall out? Why? What does it do?**

5. Optional: Go outdoors. Fill your container halfway with water. Spin it. Stop it. **What happens? Why?**

why it works

When you start to whirl your container, the container and object inside it try to keep doing what they are doing—moving in a straight line away from you! (This is called inertia.) But the container keeps the object moving in a circle as long as your hand on the string keeps whirling the container (velocity) and pulling it back toward you (centripetal force). When you stop whirling the container, gravity causes it to drop. The item stops moving too.

Prayer and Praise

God created these ways for the planets to move so that every planet has its own orbit. We're glad the moon and planets stay in their orbits! Let's name the planets of our solar system. Pray, thanking God for His universe.

DAY FOUR: Sun, Moon and Stars

Alka-Seltzer® Rocket

For every four children, gather

- Paper
- Markers
- Scissors
- Tape
- 4 dark-colored film canisters
- Water
- 2 Alka-Seltzer® tablets (broken in half)

introduce

If we were to send a rocket into space, how would we get it to blast off? Let's try this way to make gases that can blast off little rockets of our own!

Do

1. Draw, color and cut out one or two rocket shapes to tape to your film canister. Turn the canister upside down to tape shapes to its sides so that the bottom of rocket shapes are even with canister lid.

2. Fill the canister about ¼ full of water.

3. Take the canister and lid outside.

4. Drop half an Alka-Seltzer® tablet into the canister and quickly reseal the lid.

5. Set canister (lid down) on the ground. In about 30 seconds watch it blast off!

why it works

When Alka-Seltzer® reacts with water, it makes a gas. The gas built up inside the film canister until it popped like a rocket a few feet into the air. In the same way, it takes an explosion to get a rocket to blast out of our orbit so that it can go into space.

Prayer and Praise

Where would you like to go if you could explore outer space? Volunteers tell. Let's thank God for making the planets! Volunteers take turns to name planets in sentence prayers of thanks. (Optional: Students draw planet pictures and write a prayer of thanks on the picture.)

DAY FOUR: Sun, Moon and Stars

outdoor Solar Cooker

For every four children, gather

- Pizza box, cut as shown (sketch a)
- Aluminum foil
- Scissors
- Clear heavy plastic (available at hardware stores)
- Black construction paper
- Clear packing tape or duct tape
- 4 sets of S'mores ingredients: Resealable sandwich bag with a marshmallow and a piece of chocolate bar between 2 graham crackers
- Straw or pencil

introduce

How many ways of cooking have you tried? Today we're going to use the sun to cook a snack!

Do

1. Lift the cut flap in the middle of the lid. Cover it with aluminum foil, making foil as smooth as you can.

2. Cut a piece of the heavy plastic slightly larger than the opening left by the flap. This will be your oven window.

3. Lift the pizza box lid. Tape the plastic firmly to the inside of the box lid. Don't leave any air gaps.

4. With the lid still open, cover the inside bottom with aluminum foil. Cover foil with black construction paper.

5. Lay the S'mores bags inside the pizza box.

6. Close the pizza box lid and prop open the shiny flap with a straw or pencil. Face the shiny flap toward the sun. Adjust so the flap reflects as much sunlight as possible into the oven window. Observe the S'mores to see when they are ready. Enjoy!

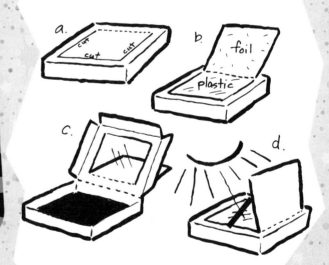

why it works

The shiny flap reflects and concentrates the sunlight through the window of the solar oven. The oven can reach temperatures of 275 degrees Fahrenheit. If you try cooking anything else in your oven, expect it to take about twice as long as it would in a conventional oven.

Prayer and Praise

How else can you use your cooker? God gave us the sun for many reasons. What are some other ways we use the sun's light? Let's thank God for every use of the sun we can think of. (Optional: Students create a mural showing uses for the sun and add a written prayer.)

DAY FIVE

Birds and Fish

"And God said, 'Let the water teem with living creatures, and let birds fly above the earth across the expanse of the sky.' So God created the great creatures of the sea and every living and moving thing with which the water teems, according to their kinds, and every winged bird according to its kind. And God saw that it was good. God blessed them and said, 'Be fruitful and increase in number and fill the water in the seas, and let the birds increase on the earth.' And there was evening, and there was morning—the fifth day."

Genesis 1:20-23

Explore the wonderful world of things that swim and fly—and the why!

DAY FIVE: Birds and Fish

Blubber Fun

For every four children, gather

- Dishpan filled halfway with water and ice
- Can of solid shortening
- Plastic food service gloves

introduce

What birds and animals live in the very cold water? (Penguins. Walruses. Seals.) **To stay warm in cold water, these birds and ocean animals have a layer of fat under their skins called blubber. Let's see how blubber keeps them warm, even in very cold water.**

Do

1. Children take turns to slide a food service glove over one hand and place that hand in the shortening can. Invite child to wiggle hand to coat the glove with shortening.

2. Child puts both hands into the water. **How does the hand covered in "blubber" feel compared to the hand without it?**

why it works

The shortening that coats the glove makes a barrier against the cold. We call it insulation. The hands that have no insulation get very cold very quickly!

Prayer and Praise

God made a way for animals to stay warm in very cold water. What are ways God helps us to stay warm? (Clothing. Houses. Heaters.) **God loves us. He takes good care of everything He has made.** Invite each child to stand as you say, **(Henry) thanks God for keeping us warm.** Continue until all children have had a turn. (Optional: Children draw a picture of a way God shows His love. Add dictated prayers to the pictures.)

DAY FIVE: Birds and Fish

ocean Sounds

For a large group, gather

• Pictures of underwater scenes that include fish and undersea mammals

• CD of underwater sounds (whale calls, dolphin chirps, etc.) and player

introduce

God made many creatures that live under the ocean. Today we'll see if we can guess what sounds each of these undersea creatures makes.

Do

1. Show pictures of underwater scenes. Children name creatures and items in the picture.

2. Play the CD. Children try to identify sounds they hear, pointing to creatures that they think are making the sounds.

why it works

We cannot usually hear the sounds undersea creatures make. But they do make sounds. Some of their calls can be heard for miles and miles under the water! This recording helps us know what their calls and songs sound like.

Prayer and Praise

What does it sound like when you call for (your mom)? Children respond. What does it sound like when we sing a song to thank God? Lead children in a song of thanks ("God Is So Good") to sing as a prayer. (Optional: Children draw an undersea mural and dictate words of a prayer to be read aloud.)

DAY FIVE: Birds and Fish

Bird talk

For every eight children, gather

- One or more objects having to do with birds (live bird in a cage, feathers, birdseed, bird's nest, pictures of birds and nests, etc.)

- Optional—audiocassette recorder and tape

introduce

Where are some places you see birds? Today we are going to talk about birds and the sounds birds make.

Do

1. Children examine the bird-related items. Which of these items help people take care of a bird? What can you learn about birds by looking at the items?

2. Children think about the sounds birds make and then take turns to make different bird sounds (caw like a crow, cluck like a chicken, hoot like an owl, crow like a rooster, coo like a dove, etc.).

3. Optional: Record sounds on the cassette recorder. When everyone has had a turn, replay tape. What bird sound do you hear? Who made that sound?

why it works

Different kinds of birds each have their own calls and songs. Besides that, each kind of bird has a different call to say hello, to warn others of danger and to find each other.

Prayer and Praise

If you were a bird, what would you want to praise God for making? Children respond. Let's all pretend to be birds. We'll flap our wings and take turns to say, "Thank You, God, for (sky)!" (Optional: Children glue feathers to bird outlines printed on paper and dictate a prayer that a teacher reads aloud.)

DAY FIVE: Birds and Fish

texture touch

For every four children, gather

- Fish scales (from a fish market or scraped from a partially-thawed frozen fish)

- Bird feathers

- Suction-cup strips cut from a rubber bath mat

- Dishpan half full of water

introduce

What is on the outside of fish? What do birds have on the outside? What is on the outside of octopus or starfish that help them hold on to things? Let's explore these outside parts.

Do

1. Children look at fish scales. **Fish scales grow rings (raised ridges) every year. Count the rings on one scale. How old was the fish?**

2. Look at the feathers. **How are long and straight (flight) feathers different from soft, fluffy (down) feathers? Which are on birds' wings? Which keep birds warm?**

3. Explore the suction cup strips. **How can you make them stick to your arm?**

4. Dip the suction cup strips into water. **What makes them stick better?**

why it works

We don't have a live fish, bird or octopus. But we can touch these items to learn about what these creatures are like on the outside. What does a bird use to hold on? What does an octopus use? How does a fish hold on?

Prayer and Praise

What do we have on the outsides of our bodies? Children respond. **What would we look like without skin? Let's thank God for making feathers, scales, suction cups and skin to protect the creatures He made!** Volunteers say a sentence prayer, thanking God for any of these coverings. (Optional: Children paint birds and fish on a mural, adding scales and feathers as desired or dipping suction-cup strips into paint to make prints. Volunteers pray sentence prayers while children work on mural.)

DAY FIVE: Birds and Fish

watery world Graph

For every four children, gather

- Plastic toy fish and sea creatures
- Paper
- Marker
- Fish crackers
- Blocks
- Blue construction paper

introduce

The Bible tells us that God made oceans and rivers and then He made wonderful fish to swim in the oceans and rivers. Today we're going to make graphs that show us how many sea creatures we have in our collection.

Do

1. Invite children to sort toy fish and sea creatures by kind, color or size.

2. After children have sorted sea creatures, invite them to graph each category by drawing a column on paper for each category and then using fish crackers as markers on the graph.

3. Discuss the graph. **Which category has the most? The least?**

4. Children use blocks and blue construction paper to outline oceans or rivers and then play with toy fish and sea creatures.

why it works

God made fish in many kinds and colors. Some fish are large and some are tiny. Some fish live in fresh water, like a river or a stream. Other fish live in salt water, in the ocean.

Prayer and Praise

God made many, many kinds of fish. What kind of fish would you like to be? Children respond. **Let's all act like the kinds of fish we want to be!** Lead children in a prayer of thanks. (Optional: Children brush tempera paint onto fish and press fish onto paper to make fish prints. Add a written prayer and read it aloud.)

DAY FIVE: Birds and Fish

Nesting Instinct

For every four children, gather

- 4 paper lunch bags
- Optional—paper and glue

Introduce

What do birds do when they want to build a nest? Where do you think they find the items they need to build nests? Today let's pretend to be birds and look for things we could use to build a nest.

Do

1. Give each child a paper lunch bag and take children for a nature walk outdoors.

2. While on the nature walk, children look for items a bird might use to build a nest—grass, twigs, bits of thread or fabric, leaves, etc. **Pick up nesting materials and place them in your bag.**

3. When children have finished the walk, help children fold down the tops of their bags so that the nesting materials can be seen. Children set their bags outdoors near trees so that they can watch to see if birds discover the bags and take the nesting materials. **What items do the birds take?**

4. Optional: After the bags have been outside for a day or two, bring in the leftover materials. Glue materials to paper to make bird's nest pictures.

why it works

Each kind of bird builds its nest in a different way. Some birds use more twigs. Some birds use more grasses. Many birds pull out their softest feathers to make a soft place for their eggs.

Prayer and Praise

God made birds able to build special kinds of nests. What did God make you able to do? Children respond. Let's thank God for the things He made us able to do. Let's all clap our hands and say, "Thank You, God." Invite a volunteer to suggest another action to do while repeating the prayer. (Optional: Children make nest pictures as above and then dictate prayers to add to pictures.)

DAY FIVE: Birds and Fish

Rise and Dive

For every four children, gather

- Dishpan half full of water
- 4 to 6 empty plastic water or soda bottles

introduce

Where do fish live? God made fish able to swim and breathe underwater through openings called gills. Let's think about how fish swim up and down. Then we'll see how we can make some things float higher or lower in the water.

Do

1. Children completely fill some plastic bottles with water, fill some partially and leave some empty.

2. Children try floating the different bottles. **Why do some of the bottles sink? Why do some float on top of the water? Why do some float under the surface?**

why it works

The bottles we filled and partly filled show us how fish move up and down. Fish store air in a place called a swim bladder. When more air is in the swim bladder, the fish moves upward in the water. When less air is in the swim bladder, the fish moves downward.

Prayer and Praise

What do you like best to do in the water? Let's thank God for ways we enjoy water. Volunteers take turns to pantomime an action done in water for others to guess. When action is guessed all say, **Thank You, God, for (swimming).** (Optional: Children make a mural including fish and children playing in water, each dictating a short prayer to add to the mural.)

Aquarium in a Bag

For every child, gather

- Gallon-sized resealable plastic bag
- Aquarium pebbles or colored paper
- Precut magazine pictures of fish and underwater items
- Paper
- Markers
- Scissors
- Short lengths of string
- Tape

introduce

What do you see when you look inside an aquarium? Today we will each make our own aquariums—but without water!

Do

1. Child opens a resealable bag and drops aquarium gravel or bits of colored paper in the bottom.

2. Child selects magazine pictures of fish and aquarium life or draws and cuts out pictures.

3. Child tapes cutouts to short lengths of string and then tapes ends of strings inside bag as desired.

4. Child tells about his or her aquarium. **What could you tell someone about the fish in your aquarium? Do your fish have names? What do they eat?**

why it works

There are some kinds of fish that can live in aquariums. They are often small and brightly colored. Some aquariums hold salt water, like we find in the ocean. Other aquariums hold fresh water, like we find in lakes. A fish that is born in fresh water usually cannot live a long time in salt water. And a fish born in salt water usually cannot live a long time in fresh water. Their bodies are made for the places they were born.

Prayer and Praise

Name something that God made to live in the (ocean) water. Now name something God made to live in the (fresh) water. Volunteers take turns to tell. Then invite volunteers to include their ideas as all say, **Thank You, God, for (seaweed).** (Optional: Children dictate short prayers to be taped to the outsides of their aquarium bags.)

DAY FIVE: Birds and Fish

Bird Bone Building

For every eight children, gather

- Boiled, dried chicken or turkey bones (add a little lemon juice to boiling water to whiten bones)

- Optional—vinegar

Introduce

When have you seen bird bones? How big are the bones inside birds? Today we will investigate some bird bones to learn more about them.

Do

1. Invite children to look at the bones. **What shapes are they? Do you think they look like any bones you might have?**

2. Children try breaking a small bone in half. **What does the bone look like on the inside? Do you think your bones look the same on the inside?**

3. Children try hooking the bones together. **What bones seem to fit with other bones? What bones can you put together?**

4. Optional: After examining bones, cover them in vinegar. Let the bones sit for three to four days. **What happens to the bones?** Let children examine.

why it works

Birds have bones that are lighter than human bones. They have more air spaces in them. Having these lighter bones makes it easier for birds to fly.

Prayer and Praise

Let's pretend to fly like birds. Now let's find a branch to sit on. Children sit on floor. Dear God, thank You for the beautiful birds You made! In Jesus' name, amen. (Optional: Children use glue to attach feathers to paper for bird pictures. Pray aloud with children.)

Pill Bug Walk

For every child, gather

- Paper cup
- Optional—small blocks or dominoes

introduce

Where do you think we could find pill bugs? Today we will find some and explore with them!

Do

1. Children take paper cups and go on a nature walk. To find a pill bug, try looking where there are old pieces of wood or rocks on the ground. Move dead leaves and twigs to find one. Each child scoops up a pill bug in cup.

2. Invite children to put the pill bugs in their hands. **It won't bite or sting. How does it feel? What does it look like? What color is your pill bug? Is it a different color from someone else's? Which pill bug is the largest?**

3. Optional: Use the small blocks or dominoes to outline a track or maze for pill bugs. **Does the pill bug follow the track? Where does it like to stop?**

4. Put pill bugs back right where they were found. **The pill bugs need to go home.**

why it works

Pill bugs live nearly everywhere. They like to live where it is moist. They eat dead leaves, plants and wood. They clean things up and help to make good soil. Pill bugs are also food for birds!

Prayer and Praise

Birds eat pill bugs and many other things, too. What things do you like to eat? Children tell. Invite them to repeat prayer, phrase by phrase, after you, first in a whisper, and then louder, and then in outdoor voices. **Dear God, thank You for making food for birds to eat. Thank You for making food for us to eat. We love You! In Jesus' name, amen.** (Optional: Children pretend to be birds looking for food as you repeat the prayer together.)

DAY FIVE: Birds and Fish

Chicken Clucker

For every child, gather

- Paper cup with a small hole poked in its bottom
- 2-foot (.6-m) length of cotton string
- Water in a shallow container

Introduce

Chickens are birds that live on farms. What do you know about chickens? Today we will make something that will sound like a chicken clucking!

Do

1. Instruct each child to run a length of string through the hole in the bottom of cup, and then pull the string out the top of the cup.

2. With adult help, child ties a knot that is too big to fit through the hole.

3. When the knot is finished, the string should hang from the bottom of the cup.

4. Child dips the string in water. **Holding the cup in one hand, use your thumb and forefinger to pull on the wet string, a little at a time. What does it do? What do you think it sounds like?**

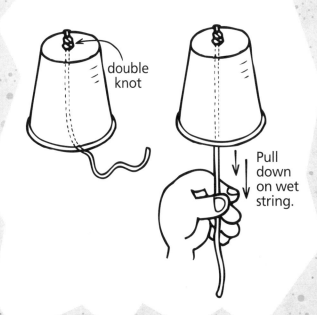

double knot

Pull down on wet string.

Why it Works

When the string is wet, it stops our fingers. (That is called friction.) When our fingers stop, it makes the string vibrate. It makes a sound like a chicken clucking!

Prayer and Praise

How do chickens move? Show me! Children bob, flap and walk like chickens. **Let's all pretend to be chickens sitting on our nests as we thank God for making chickens!** Pray, inviting children to repeat after you, phrase by phrase. (Optional: Children draw a barnyard scene with chickens across large butcher paper. Add a prayer of thanks along the bottom of the picture.)

DAY FIVE: Birds and Fish

Fossil Finds

For every four children, gather
- Purchased or homemade dough
- Boiled, dry bones from chickens and fish

introduce

Scientists often find the marks left by bones and other things. They are called fossils. Today we will make our own fossils and play a game with them!

Do

1. Children make balls of dough and then flatten them.

2. Children press several bones into the dough. **If you want, lay another flattened ball of dough over the top, press and then pull it off to make two "fossil rocks."**

3. When everyone in the group has made several "fossil rocks," trade them with others in your group. **Figure out which bones were used to make this fossil. Is it easy or hard to match the bones to the empty spaces left on the fossil?**

why it works

When we press the bones into the dough, it is something like what happened when a fossil was made. God made birds, fish and other animals long ago. We can still see their fossil impressions in rocks today. A real fossil is the shape of the bones of an animal that died and was covered by mud. As the mud became rock, the shapes of the animal's bones were left in the rock! Plants, shells and other things can become fossils, too.

Prayer and Praise

What animal fossils would you like to find? Children tell. **Let's thank God for amazing rocks He made!** Invite children to repeat after you, phrase by phrase. **Thank You, God, for rocks and bones. Thank You, God, for fossil stones. Thank You, God, for loving me. Thank You, God, for all I see.** (Optional: Write prayer in the center of paper for children to illustrate.)

DAY FIVE: Birds and Fish

Floating on Lift

For every child, gather

- Plastic funnel
- Table tennis ball

introduce

How is it that birds are able to fly? God made air so that it is possible for birds (and also for airplanes) to lift off the ground and fly. Let's see how it works!

Do

1. Hold the funnel upside down.

2. Bend over and put the small end of the funnel in your mouth. Blow through the funnel so that the air goes straight down.

3. Now hold the table tennis ball inside the large end of the funnel.

4. Start blowing. Then let go of the table tennis ball. **What happens?**

why it works

The ball floats inside the funnel because the air passing by it is moving quickly. This puts less pressure above the ball than the air pressure under the ball. Since the air pressure is greater below the ball than the pressure is above it, the ball is held in the air! We call this upward push "lift."

Prayer and Praise

When air moves over a bird's wing, it moves faster over the top than over the bottom surface. What other things use this rule about how air works? (Kites. Paper airplanes. Hang gliders.) **God designed every detail of our world in a good way. Let's thank Him!** Invite several volunteers to say sentence prayers of thanks that include some of the items students mentioned. (Optional: Draw pictures of things that fly. Cut out and attach pictures to strings. Hang them from light fixtures or ceiling.)

DAY FIVE: Birds and Fish

Bug watcher

For every child, gather

• Clear plastic, disposable cup with lid, with a pencil-sized hole in its bottom

• 4" length of plastic tubing, or an extra-wide straw

• Half of a drinking straw

• Small piece of gauze

• Rubber bands

• Masking tape

introduce

What are some important things that insects do? (Pollinate plants. Are food for animals, birds, fish, reptiles.) **Here's a way to easily watch and learn about insects!**

Do

1. Cover one end of the straw piece with gauze. Secure it with a rubber band.

2. Work the other end of the straw through the hole in the bottom of the cup from the inside.

3. Wrap a rubber band around the straw where it sticks out of the bottom to hold it in place.

4. Work the plastic tubing through the hole in the lid of the cup. If it is loose, wrap a rubber band on the tubing both above and below the lid to secure it.

5. Use masking tape wherever needed to make an air-tight seal.

6. Put the lid on securely. Now you're ready to go outdoors on an insect observer's hunt!

why it works

The gauze will keep you from sucking up any insects. By sucking gently, you should be able to bring an insect inside the cup to watch it. When you are finished, just open the lid and release it.

Prayer and Praise

How many kinds of insects can you name? Students tell. **Think of one kind of insect. When I pause while we pray, say the name of that insect!** (Optional: Students make model insects from recyclable materials and write prayers on models.)

Fish Floaties

For every four children, gather

- Bowl of water
- 6 to 12 condiment (ketchup, mustard, soy sauce) packets
- Four 2-liter soda bottles with caps, each nearly filled with water

introduce

Why do you think a fish can swim up and down under water, yet not float to the top? Let's do an experiment to find out.

Do

1. Drop condiment packets into a bowl of water. Select a packet that floats.

2. Place inside your bottle of water the packet you chose. Screw on the cap tightly.

3. Grab the bottle with both hands. Squeeze the bottle. **Which way does the packet move?**

4. Release the bottle. **Which direction does the packet move?**

5. Remove the first packet. Put a different packet into your bottle. Squeeze. **Does the second packet sink and rise more easily? Why or why not?**

why it works

A bubble of air is sealed inside each packet. It is like a fish's swim bladder (an air-filled sac at the dorsal side, or top, of its body). When you are not squeezing the bottle, the packet floats higher because the bubble of air is larger. When you squeeze the bottle, you increase pressure inside the bottle. This pressure compresses the air bubble, making the packet denser so it sinks. This is the way many kinds of fish control their buoyancy (ability to float underwater). So do submarines!

Prayer and Praise

Where do you think people got the idea for how to make a submarine dive? (From fish.) What are some other inventions people have made that might have come from watching birds or fish? (Airplanes. Rudders. Suction cups.) Let's each thank God for a creature that lives under water. Students take turns to pray sentence prayers. (Optional: Students draw inventions and then tape illustrations together to make a "row of inventions.")

DAY FIVE: Birds and Fish

Feather Flight!

For every four children, gather

- Bird's flight feather (long feather)
- Push pin
- Stick or ruler
- Handheld hair dryer (blow-dryer)

introduce

How long was the longest feather you've ever seen? What part of the bird was it from? Let's find out how both small and large birds use their feathers to fly!

Do

1. Attach the feather to the stick by pushing the pin through the feather's shaft where the barbs (the little parts that make a feather) end. Be sure that the shorter barbs are pointing down.

2. Have a partner stand the stick up and hold it steady. Test the feather to be sure it moves freely on the pin.

3. Ask a friend to stand near the barbless end of the feather, point the hair dryer at the feather and turn the dryer on (cool setting). **What happens?**

4. Blow air from different angles. **At which angle does the feather lift upward?**

why it works

We see how one feather lifts when air moves past it. Imagine what happens when rows of these lifters work together! God gave birds flight feathers and made many of a bird's bones hollow so it can fly easily!

Prayer and Praise

God designed flight feathers just so birds can fly. He designed down feathers to keep birds warm. What's a part of you God designed so that you could praise Him? (Eyes to look at His creation. Mind to think. Mouth to sing.) **Let's add those ways to our prayer. Begin, Dear God, thank You for making our (hands) so we can praise You by . . .** Volunteers insert a way to use hands to praise God. (Optional: Students outline a body on butcher paper and illustrate ways they can use their body parts to praise God.)

DAY FIVE: Birds and Fish

Shells of Lime

For every four children, gather

- Clear glass half full of vinegar
- 3 to 4 seashells
- Several small rocks

Introduce

What are some differences between seashells and rocks? What do you think seashells are made of? Let's see if we can find out.

Do

1. Place a seashell in the glass of vinegar. Watch to see what happens.

2. Add another shell and then another. **Does each shell react in the same way?**

3. Add a rock to the vinegar. **Does the rock react as the shells did? Why do you think this happens?**

Why it works

Vinegar is an acid. When it touches lime, it reacts by giving off gas bubbles. Lime is the mineral seashells are made of. Limestone is also in some rocks, so some rocks might also give off gas bubbles. God made many creatures that are able to grow (secrete) shells, just as He made us able to grow fingernails. What undersea creatures secrete lime to make hard shells? (Snails. Limpets. Clams. Mussels. Crabs. Lobsters.)

Prayer and Praise

As some undersea creatures (like crabs) grow, their old shells come off. They usually hide until they grow larger shells. Let's thank God for the variety of undersea creatures He made. Lead children in prayer. (Optional: Students make an undersea mural that includes shelled undersea creatures and add a written prayer.)

DAY FIVE: Birds and Fish

Glider wings

For every four children, gather
- 8 to 12 sheets of plain paper

introduce

When birds fly, we can see that they often glide on the air. Let's try making some gliders of our own to help us understand how birds glide.

Do

1. Fold your paper in any way you usually do to make a paper airplane.

2. Work together to make each airplane or glider in a slightly different way from the others in your group.

3. Trade and test the gliders by flying them. **Which glider travels farthest or highest? Which one can glide in loops? Which one flies a short distance?**

4. Compare: **What causes the gliders to fly in different ways?**

why it works

Like our different gliders, various kinds of birds' wings are of many shapes and sizes. Each kind of bird flies differently: Hummingbirds flap short, tapered wings nearly all the time! Birds with long wings (like pelicans) make long strokes in the air. When birds don't have to flap their wings, it saves their energy, so birds that are able to glide, glide often. These birds also do what scientists call "kiting"—hanging in the air, supported by updrafts (thermals) that are caused by changes in land temperature.

Prayer and Praise

Our gliders are not nearly as amazing as the birds God made. Birds not only fly but also glide and kite—and are able to take off and land! Invite each student to thank God for a different kind of bird.

144

DAY FIVE: Birds and Fish

Hold on tight

For every four children, gather

- Variety of rocks (some smooth, some rough)
- Four suction cups (such as the type available at craft stores for hanging a craft on a window)
- Dishpan containing water

Introduce

If you went to the ocean or an aquarium, you would see many creatures clinging to rocks. Let's discover how they can hold on so tightly!

Do

1. Push a suction cup onto a rock. **Can you lift the rock with the suction cup?**

2. Dip your suction cup in water and then push it onto a rock. **Is it easier or harder to lift?**

3. Keep on testing. **Which rock is easiest to pick up? Why do you think so?**

4. Put a rock in the water. **Can you lift the underwater rock with the suction cup?**

Suction Cup
Rock

why it works

Pushing a suction cup onto a rock forces the air out of the cup. The water forms a seal around the outside edge so that air can't get back inside. The air in the room also pushes on the outside of the cup to help hold the cup tightly to the rock. Anemones and some other clinging creatures have structures like suction cups (called a pedal disc) on their rock-holding ends! Their pedal discs are held tight by the pressure of the water.

Prayer and Praise

What are some other undersea creatures that use suction cups? (Octopus. Starfish.) Let's thank God for as many of these kinds of undersea creatures as we can think of. Students take turns to say a sentence prayer, including the name of a creature that has structures like a suction cup. (Optional: Students paint a mural of an undersea scene, dipping suction cups into tempera to make prints, and add a written prayer.)

DAY FIVE: Birds and Fish

wave Bottles

For every four children, gather

- Small clear plastic water bottle, half full of mineral oil
- Blue food coloring
- Funnel
- Water
- Electrical tape
- Optional—a book illustrating the tidal zones near the ocean

introduce

God created life that lives in the ocean but He also made many other creatures that live at the edge of the ocean. They live in what are called the tidal zones. While we make our wave bottles, let's see if we can name ocean animals that are wet only part of the time. (Optional: Children use the book illustrating tidal zones to help them see what sea creatures are not always wet.)

Do

1. Add a few drops of food coloring to the bottle.

2. Pour water through the funnel to fill the bottle with water.

3. Replace the cap. Wrap electrical tape tightly around the cap to seal it.

4. Tip the bottle back and forth horizontally to watch the wave action.

why it works

These waves are easy to see because mineral oil always floats on top of the water. It keeps the waves from splashing. Many ocean creatures live under water all the time. Which ocean animals must go to the top of the water? (Dolphins. Porpoises. Whales. Sea lions.) Why? What animals did God make to live where they are wet some of the time? (Crabs. Snails. Limpets. Barnacles.)

Prayer and Praise

Think of your favorite animal that lives in or near the ocean. When I say, "Thank You, God, for . . . ." say the name of the animal you thought of.

DAY SIX

Animals and People

"And God said, 'Let the land produce living creatures according to their kinds: livestock, creatures that move along the ground, and wild animals, each according to its kind.' And it was so. God made the wild animals according to their kinds, the livestock according to their kinds, and all the creatures that move along the ground according to their kinds. And God saw that it was good. Then God said, 'Let us make man in our image, in our likeness, and let them rule over the fish of the sea and the birds of the air, over the livestock, over all the earth, and over all the creatures that move along the ground.'"
Genesis 1:24-26

Here are experiments that explore the wonderful ways in which God made animals—and us!

DAY SIX: Animals and People

Fingerprint Fun

For every four children, gather

- Several magnifying glasses
- White paper
- Washable inkpad
- Premoistened towelettes

introduce

How many of you have (blue) eyes? Who has (brown) hair? There is one part of you that is different from what anyone else has. Today you can explore that part of you!

Do

1. Children use magnifying glasses to examine fingertips.

2. Children make fingerprints on white paper by pressing fingers on inkpad and then on the paper.

3. Children clean hands with towelettes after making fingerprints.

4. Use a magnifying glass to compare your paper fingerprints with other's fingerprints. How do your prints look different from another person's? What is the same about both sets of fingerprints?

why it works

Every fingerprint is different. No one else has the same fingerprint pattern as you do. Your fingerprints show that you can't be confused with anyone else.

Prayer and Praise

What else is special about the way God made you? Our voices are not like anyone else's, either. Let's use them to praise God for making us special! Children select and sing a song of thanks to God as a prayer. (Optional: Children listen to songs of praise to God while drawing a picture and then dictate prayers to add to paper.)

DAY SIX: Animals and People

Smell well

For every four children, gather

- Variety of scented food items (lemon, orange, chocolate, tuna, vinegar, spaghetti sauce, bubble gum, banana, spices, etc.)

- Small film or dairy containers with lids

- Cotton balls

introduce

God gave each of us a nose. What does your nose do? Let's find out more about one way we use our noses!

Do

1. Place pieces of solid food items in containers. For liquids, place cotton balls in containers and add a bit of liquid. Place lids on containers.

2. Children take turns to close eyes while a partner removes a container lid and holds container for person with closed eyes to sniff and guess what the scent is. (Note: If the smells are very concentrated, remove the lid a moment before sniffing the contents.)

3. For another round, smell and tell the name of something else that smells like that item.

why it works

God made people and animals able to smell very well! We can tell many things by smelling. Some animals are much better at smelling than we are. Dogs learn most of what they know by smelling!

Prayer and Praise

What is your favorite smell? When I say your name, you can say your favorite smell in our prayer. Pray, **God, (Lisa) is glad for (flowers). That's (her) favorite smell!** (Optional: Children draw pictures of items they enjoy smelling. Add pictures to a bulletin board and add a written prayer to the middle of the display.)

DAY SIX: Animals and People

Measure Up

For every two children, gather
- Construction paper
- Marker
- Scissors
- Optional—measuring tape

introduce

How big is your hand? How long is your foot? Let's experiment with finding out what else in the room is the same length as your (foot).

Do

1. Partners take turns to trace around each other's hand or foot on a sheet of construction paper. Child cuts around own hand or foot shape.

2. Child uses the hand or foot shape to compare with objects in the room that are as long as the child's hand or foot.

3. **Find objects in the room longer or shorter than your hand or foot shape.**

4. Lay all the prints in a row. **Which print is the longest? The widest? The shortest?**

5. Optional: Help children use a measuring tape to determine the exact sizes of the prints.

why it works

God made us to grow. Our feet and hands are bigger than they were last year. Everyone's body grows just the way God wants it to. That is the reason some feet and hands are bigger, some smaller. Each person is different and God says that is good!

Prayer and Praise

Let's thank God for His love and for making us grow. When I say your name, stand and say, "Thank You, God." Pray, **God, You are good to help us grow.** Then call each child by name to add to the prayer. Close, **In Jesus' name, amen.** (Optional: Children glue prints to large butcher paper and color to make a mural. Add a written prayer.)

DAY SIX: Animals and People

Sorting Animals

For every four children, gather

- Cardboard boxes or paper plates, labeled "Home," "Zoo," "Jungle," "Other Places," etc.

- Toy animals or magazine pictures of animals

introduce

Animals live in many kinds of places. Some animals live in our homes as pets. Some animals visit our homes, like birds. Show children the boxes or plates. Read labels aloud. **Let's sort these animals by the place they live.**

Do

Children sort the toy animals or pictures of animals according to where the animals live, placing animals in the appropriate boxes or on the appropriate plates. Children sort animals according to the category labels on the other boxes or plates.

why it works

God made animals to live in many kinds of places. Some live in dry deserts and some in wet swamps. Some live in forests and some in apartments where there are no trees at all!

Prayer and Praise

God made many wonderful animals! Let's each name an animal God made. Children respond. Then pray, **Thank You, God, for all these animals. In Jesus' name, amen.** (Optional: Children draw pictures of animals and then show pictures as they name animals.)

DAY SIX: Animals and People

Listen to the Sounds

For every four children, gather

- 2 each of a variety of small items (gravel, marbles, cotton balls, pasta, paper clips, buttons, jingle bells, etc.)
- Several clean, small yogurt containers with lids
- Masking tape

introduce

What sounds do you hear when you are outside? In a store? Today we'll play a detective game using our ears!

Do

1. Ahead of time, place one kind of item in each container, reserving other item of each kind. Place lids on containers and tape lids securely.

2. Children take turns shaking containers one at a time to guess what item might be inside each container.

3. Show the items you reserved. Children shake containers again, trying to match sounds from the containers with the items.

4. After children have guessed, open containers to reveal items.

why it works

God made our ears so that we hear many kinds of sounds. We can hear the rolling sound of a marble and the jingling sound of a bell. We can tell if an item is hard or soft, large or small, by the sound it makes when it hits the container.

Prayer and Praise

God made our ears to hear. Let's play an add-on game, naming something we can hear. First child names an item. Second child names the first item and another item. Third child names first two and one more, and so on. Begin a new round after five items have been listed. End by saying, **Thank You, God, for all we can hear!** (Optional: Children list items whose sounds they can hear and then illustrate the list, ending by reading list aloud and praying.)

DAY SIX: Animals and People

Hiding Animals

For every eight children, gather

- Variety of small plastic animals
- Construction paper in earth tones (brown, gray, white, green, tan)

Introduce

What's a place you like to hide? Animals hide, too. Let's play a game to think about how some kinds of animals hide so that they can stay safe!

Do

1. Lay out sheets of construction paper.

2. Children take turns to select a plastic animal. Others guess on which color of paper the animal would most easily be hidden.

3. Child sets his or her animal on chosen color of paper to see if the animal would be well hidden there.

4. Where does each animal live? In a tan or brown desert? In a green forest? On a gray mountain? Why do you think God made the animal the color that it is? How does the animal's color help it to hide?

why it works

God made animals in many different colors. Their color often helps them hide safely in their homes. If a (polar bear) tried to hide in (green grass), would it be easy or hard to see? What if the (polar bear) tried to hide in a (snowy) place? Animals' markings and colors help them hide and stay safe!

Prayer and Praise

How many (green) animals can you name? Let's thank God for (green) animals He made. We'll say, "Thank You, God" and wait so you can say the name of the animal. Continue with other colors as time and interest permit. (Optional: Children draw a mural of an environment and its animals and then dictate a prayer to add to the mural.)

DAY SIX: Animals and People

Animal tracks

For every four children, gather

- Wet or dry sand

- Items that will make prints like animal tracks in the sand (forks, cotton balls, twigs, small spatulas, corks, etc.)

- Optional—illustrations of animal tracks from nature books or the Internet, animal track stencils and paint or sidewalk chalk

Introduce

If we were looking for wild animals in the places they live, what clues might we look for to find them? (Homes. Tracks.) Today let's make some animal tracks of our own.

Do

1. Children press items into sand, experimenting with ways to make tracks resembling those of different animals. (Optional: Show illustrations of animal tracks.)

2. Optional: Children hold stencils of animal tracks in place on sidewalk and use paint or sidewalk chalk to create paths of animal tracks.

why it works

Every kind of animal has its own footprint or track. God made animals and people with different kinds of tracks! What does your track look like?

Prayer and Praise

God gave us feet to walk. How many feet do we walk on? How many feet do (tigers) walk on? Let's get down on all fours and walk like animals and then thank God for our feet! (Optional: Children use paint and animal track materials to make an animal track mural, adding a dictated prayer to thank God for feet.)

DAY SIX: Animals and People

texture walk

For every four children, gather

• Variety of materials with different textures (cardboard, velvet fabric, plastic place mat, carpet square, towels, bubble wrap, newspaper, sandpaper, etc.)

Introduce

What is something that feels soft? Hard? Let's see how well your feet can feel things.

Do

1. Either arrange the different materials ahead of time to create a path through the room or invite children to arrange the path themselves.

2. Children remove shoes and socks to walk bare-foot on the path. **Describe how each material feels. Is it scratchy? Soft?**

3. Now try covering eyes to walk across a texture. **What do your feet tell you about what you are touching?**

why it works

Our brains remember many kinds of information. When we touch something, our brains remember what that item felt like so that the next time we touch it, we know what it is we are touching!

Prayer and Praise

Stand in a circle, holding hands. **Let's pass a hand squeeze around our circle. When you feel your neighbor gently squeeze your hand, gently squeeze the hand of your other neighbor. I will begin. When the squeeze comes back to me, we'll thank God for making our hands and feet.** (Optional: Children glue small texture scraps onto butcher paper to create a texture mural. Add a written prayer of thanks to mural.)

DAY SIX: Animals and People

Group Graph

For every eight children, gather

- Length of butcher paper
- Masking tape
- Marker
- Optional—8 lengths of butcher paper about the length of children's height

introduce

Each person in our group is different from every other person. Let's make a graph that tells about each of us.

Do

1. Secure butcher paper to the wall with masking tape.

2. Make a graph by writing each child's name down the side of the paper and then drawing columns labeled, "straight," "curly," "wavy," "long" and "short."

3. Compare hair characteristics, inviting children to mark the graph accordingly. Graph eye colors if time allows. **What do we notice about the kinds of hair we have in our class?**

4. Optional: Children each choose a partner. On the additional lengths of butcher paper, each child draws a life-size portrait of his or her partner.

	Straight	Curly	Wavy	Long	Short
Chad		😊		😊	
Elisa			😊		😊
Lonni	😊				😊
Lily	😊			😊	
Rubio					😊

why it works

Some of us have longer hair than others. Some of us have hair that has more curl and some of us have straight hair. God made each one of us in a special way. God put messages inside every cell in our body. These messages are called DNA. The DNA tells our bodies what to do and how to grow.

Prayer and Praise

Who has the longest arms and can reach the highest? Show me! After children stretch, invite them to pray with you. Name each child as you pray. **Dear God, thank You that (Shawna, Lily, Eric and Rubio) are each different. We love You. In Jesus' name, amen.** (Optional: Children dictate prayers of thanks for their partners on partner portraits.)

Plastic tube Horn

For every child, gather

- Plastic tubing or old garden hose cut into varying lengths from 2 to 4 feet (.6 to 1.2 m)
- Plastic funnel
- Sterilized sport top from a water bottle
- Optional—other kinds of hoses (dryer vent hose, vacuum cleaner hose, etc.), musical instruments

introduce

What are some musical instruments you have seen or played? Today we will try making some musical instruments of our own!

Do

1. Child selects a length of tubing or hose and pushes a funnel into one end of the hose.

2. Child fits a water-bottle sport top onto the other end of the hose.

3. Child blows into or hums into the sport-top mouthpiece. Invite child to move the hose. **How does moving the hose change the sound?**

4. Children compare sounds with other tube horns that have shorter or longer hoses. **Do they sound the same? Different? What do you think makes them sound different?**

5. Optional: Children explore and compare other kinds of hoses and tubes to blow, sing or hum through. Provide other musical instruments to explore or invite a wind or brass instrument player to play instrument for the class.

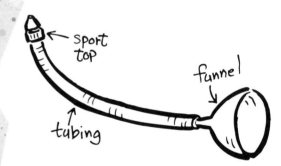

sport top

funnel

tubing

why it works

When we blow or hum through the tube, it makes a vibration. The vibration moves through the tube and makes a sound. When the hose changes shape, the sound changes, too.

Prayer and Praise

What is a musical instrument you would like to play? Let's have a praise parade and pretend to play those instruments! Children follow you, pretending to play instruments. After a parade, stop and invite volunteers to thank God for minds to think with or sounds to make. (Optional: Children record sounds made with tube horns on an audiocassette and repeat short prayers. Play back both for children and, later, for parents.)

DAY SIX: Animals and People

walk the Line

For every four children, gather

- Length of masking tape or yarn
- Optional—chalk

introduce

What parts of your body do you use when you walk? Is it easy or hard to walk on a straight line? Let's try this experiment!

Do

1. Create a straight line using masking tape or yarn. (Optional: Play game outside and draw a chalk line.)

2. Invite children to take turns walking along the line in a variety of ways: marching, tiptoeing, sliding, one foot in front of the other, etc.

why it works

We use our eyes, feet and arms when we walk. But we also use a part of our bodies we cannot see. It is deep inside our ears. It helps us keep our balance. When we move, this part keeps us from falling over. This part of our ears is filled with a liquid. When we spin around and around, we fall down because spinning sloshes that liquid around and then it can't help us keep our balance.

Prayer and Praise

God is good to make us able to keep our balance! Let's try standing on one foot while we pray. Pray, inviting children to say their names as you pause. **Dear God, (Liam) is glad he can balance.** (Optional: Provide a diagram of the inner ear. Children copy the shape onto paper. Add a written prayer of thanks for our ears.)

DAY SIX: Animals and People

Kangaroo Hop

For every four children, gather

- 4 small stuffed toy animals

- 4 long scarves

- Optional—masking tape

introduce

What do we call the place where a kangaroo carries its baby? (Pouch.) **Today we're going to pretend to be kangaroos and play a game where we carry a toy the way a kangaroo carries its baby.**

Do

1. Each child chooses a scarf and a stuffed animal. Adult folds the scarf lengthwise to make a kind of pouch. Child puts animal in the scarf pouch and then has an adult tie the scarf around child's middle.

2. Children try hopping with animals in pouches. **How does wearing a pouch feel different? Is it easier or harder to jump high? Why? What could you do to make your pouch work better?**

3. Optional: Ahead of time, lay "Start" and "Finish" lines with masking tape. Children take turns to jump to and from the finish line while wearing pouches. **You look like hopping kangaroos!** If your animal drops out of your pouch, pick it up and put it back in the pouch before hopping again.

why it works

Mammals are creatures that give birth to live babies. They feed those babies with milk. A kangaroo is a mammal. But kangaroo babies are very tiny when they are born. So they crawl into their mothers' pouches and drink milk from their mothers until they get big enough to live on their own.

Prayer and Praise

God made different kinds of mammals that move in different ways. Kangaroos hop. How do (horses) move? Show me! How do (cats) move? Continue with other mammal actions as time allows. Then invite volunteers to take turns to name a mammal in a sentence prayer. Pray, **Thank You, God, for making mammals.** Then call each child by name to add to the prayer. **(Tabitha) thanks You for making (cats).** (Optional: Children draw to make a mural of mammals they know and add written prayers.)

Early Childhood Explorations
DAY SIX: Animals and People

Animal Food Book

For every four children, gather

- 16 sandwich-sized, resealable plastic bags (4 for each child)
- 4 paper plates, each containing one of the following: grass clippings, banana chips, bits of beef jerky, variety of leaves and bark
- Stapler
- Indelible marker
- Optional—animal stickers (available at stationery stores)

Introduce

What did you eat for breakfast this morning? What do you think a (horse) might eat for breakfast? Let's make books today that we can use to tell about what animals eat.

Do

1. Children look at, touch and smell the items on each plate. **What is each food?**

2. Children put a small amount of each food into separate resealable bags. **What animals eat this kind of food? Would you eat this food?**

3. Optional: After you have talked about which animals eat each kind of food, children find a sticker of an animal that eats each kind of food and place stickers onto the correct bags.

4. Children give bags to an adult who staples them together to make a book. Children use the marker to write their names on books. **Take your book home to show your family what kinds of food animals eat.**

Why it works

God made many kinds of animals. He also made food for each one! Giraffes and elephants eat leaves and bark from tall trees. Zebras, cows and sheep eat grass. Lions and tigers eat meat. Many animals, like monkeys, eat fruit such as bananas.

Prayer and Praise

What is a food God made that you like to eat? Children tell. **Let's thank God for making food for the animals and for us!** Begin a clapping pattern for children to imitate as they repeat a prayer after you, phrase by phrase. (Optional: Children draw pictures of themselves eating a favorite food. Add a written prayer.)

DAY SIX: Animals and People

Muddy Animals

For every four children, gather

- Dishpan containing soil
- Water in a small pitcher
- Plastic toy animals

introduce

What animals like to live where there is mud? (Pigs. Ducks. Hippos.) Let's make some mud to explore while we talk about animals that like mud!

Do

1. Invite children to take turns to pour a little water into the soil.

2. Use your fingers to mix the water and the soil. How does it feel? Is it cool or warm to touch?

3. Children play with the plastic animals in the mud. If these animals were real, which ones would like being in mud? Which animals don't like mud?

why it works

Wild animals have to find water every day. If they find a water hole, it is usually in the middle of a lot of mud. So even though lions and zebras and giraffes don't stay in the mud like a pig or a hippo does, they can still get muddy. Remember how the mud felt? It felt cool. Pigs and hippos like to roll in the mud to cover up their skin. The mud helps to keep them cool in hot weather!

Prayer and Praise

What animal sound can you make? Let's take turns to make animal sounds. Children respond. Let's thank God for animals in three different ways: first, in a low voice, and then a high voice, and then a whisper. Pray using the different voices and pausing to let children repeat each phrase after you.

tasty testing

For every two children, gather

- 6 pieces of soft, bite-sized candy
- Clock or watch with a second hand
- Paper and pencil
- Optional—cow's tongue (available at butcher shops)

introduce

When you eat, what happens inside your mouth? Today, let's find the fastest way to dissolve candy in our mouths. We'll try three ways.

Do

1. Put a piece of candy in your mouth. Don't chew it or wiggle your tongue against it.

2. Look at the clock. Write down the times when you put the candy in and when it finally dissolves. **How long did it take to dissolve?**

3. Put a second piece in your mouth. This time, move the candy around with your tongue but DO NOT chew it. Record the time it takes to dissolve.

4. Put the third piece of candy in your mouth. Chew AND move it with your tongue. Record the time it takes.

5. Compare. **During which trial did the candy dissolve fastest? Why? How did the third candy taste different from the first one?**

6. Optional: Examine a cow's tongue. Notice the taste buds. **How is a cow's tongue different from yours? The same?**

why it works

Our mouths constantly make saliva. Saliva dissolves candy into a solution we can swallow. When more surfaces of the candy touch saliva, it dissolves more quickly. Moving, chewing and crushing it make more places for saliva to mix with the candy. Another reason to chew is that saliva breaks down food so that we digest it better. Our taste buds were saturated by the first piece of candy, so the third piece of candy may not have tasted as good as the first one!

Prayer and Praise

God gives us many tasty kinds of food besides candy. Let's name a food for every letter of the alphabet. Invite a volunteer to pray, thanking God for some of the foods mentioned. (Optional: Students letter the alphabet on large butcher paper and then draw pictures of foods whose names begin with each letter to create a food mural, adding written prayers.)

DAY SIX: Animals and People

touch telling

For every four children, gather
- Bible
- Variety of small items (coin, bead, eraser, etc.) inside a lunch bag

introduce

What part of your body do you use most to learn new things? Today we're going to see what we can learn without using our sense of sight. We'll use our sense of touch instead!

Do

1. Sit in a row with your hands behind your back. Set the bag behind one person.

2. With hands behind the back, person nearest the bag removes an item from the bag and feels it (without telling what it is).

3. Person then passes item behind his or her back to the next person.

4. After each person feels and passes item, the last person to feel the item holds it behind his or her back.

5. Tell what each of you think the item is. **What makes you think so?**

6. Last person shows item. **Did you guess correctly? What made it easy or hard to guess?**

7. Repeat process with other items.

A

why it works

Read Psalm 139:14 from Bible. This verse tells us we are wonderfully made. Our brains are amazing! When our hands feel the shape, texture and size of an item, our brains picture what the item might be, based on what our hands are feeling. We are wonderfully made, just like the Bible says!

Prayer and Praise

What are some other wonderful things about our bodies? Let's thank God for these wonderful bodies He made for us. I'll repeat Psalm 139:14 and then anyone who would like to may say a sentence prayer, thanking God for his or her body. (Optional: Students write out Psalm 139:14 in large letters across butcher paper and then illustrate the words as a prayer.)

DAY SIX: Animals and People

Mammal Meals

For every two children, gather

- ½ cup (.12 l) milk in a clear plastic cup
- Vinegar
- Measuring spoons
- Bowl
- Strainer
- Coffee filter

Introduce

What are your favorite things to drink? When do you drink milk? Today let's experiment to learn more about what is in milk that makes it a mammal meal.

Do

1. Measure about 4 teaspoons (20 ml) of vinegar into the cup holding the milk.

2. Watch to see what happens. If the milk doesn't change, add more vinegar.

3. Let the mixture sit for about 10 minutes.

4. Set the coffee filter in the strainer. Set the strainer over the bowl.

5. Pour the milk-and-vinegar mixture into the coffee filter. **What do you see? What do you think caused this? What does it remind you of?**

why it works

When vinegar mixes with milk, it causes a chemical reaction. The reaction causes the proteins in the milk to cling together to make what we call "curds." The liquid left behind is called "whey." Whey contains water, vitamins, minerals and other kinds of proteins. God made some creatures able to feed milk to their young. What are those creatures called? (Mammals.) All mammal babies drink milk. Even humans do! That's the reason that when you drink a glass of milk, it stops hunger pangs—it's really drinkable food.

Prayer and Praise

What are some other creatures that give milk? (Goats. Camels. Sheep.) **Let's thank God for as many mammals as we can name.** Students take turns to complete this sentence prayer: "Thank You, God, for . . . " (Optional: Students paint designs with milk on white bread and then toast bread in a toaster oven to reveal designs. Students thank God and snack on toast.)

DAY SIX: Animals and People

Bouncing Sounds

For every four children, gather

- Large bowl
- Plastic wrap
- Tape
- Salt
- Pan with lid

introduce

How many kinds of waves are there? (Ocean. Light. Sound.) People and animals have ears that work in similar ways. We can hear and sometimes feel sound waves. But today let's "see" how sound waves affect our eardrums!

Do

1. Stretch a piece of plastic wrap tightly over the top of the bowl.

2. Tape the wrap so that it is tight, like a drum.

3. Sprinkle a small amount of salt on the stretched plastic wrap.

4. Stand a few feet (about a meter) from the bowl. Holding the pot and lid at the height of the bowl, bang the lid onto the pan a few times. **What do you see happening?**

why it works

Sound waves are vibrations that move the air. The moving air moved the plastic, which bounced the salt so that we could see the vibration's effects. Our eardrums work in the same way—they bounce to the vibrations that come through the air. That's a chain reaction!

Prayer and Praise

What are some other chain reactions God made in our bodies? (Thirst makes us drink, digest, and move water to our cells. Hunger makes us eat, digest, move energy to cells and excrete waste.) **Let's thank God for as many of these chain reactions as we can name.** Students take turns to complete this sentence prayer: "Thank You, God, for . . . and . . ."

DAY SIX: Animals and People

Animal Camo

Introduce

Animals are often colored and marked in such a way that they blend with their surroundings. How does that help an animal? Today, we're going to see how good we can be at blending in to the background!

Do

1. *Teacher: Use masking tape to secure lengths of animal-print fabric to the wall at students' eye level.*

2. Choose the print you plan to match. Use the face paint and a mirror to see if you can make your face as much like the fabric as possible.

3. To test your camouflage face, stand in front of the fabric you chose and have your photo taken. **How well did your face blend in to the background? What else could you do to blend in to the background?**

4. *Teacher: If time permits, print out the photos and invite students to attach them to the fabrics that match them.*

Why it works

When animals blend in to their surroundings, it keeps them safe from predators, animals who are likely to eat them. For instance, when zebras stand together in a herd, their many stripes confuse even the sharp eyes of a lion or tiger. As long as a zebra stays with its herd, the many stripes keep a predator from seeing where one zebra ends and another begins!

Prayer and Praise

Camouflage can save people's lives, too. Soldiers sometimes paint their faces for the same reason. Let's try some voice camouflage as we pray. Anyone who wants to pray a sentence prayer may do so. But you must pray using a voice that sounds different from your normal voice! I'll pray last—in a normal voice.

DAY SIX: Animals and People

center of Gravity Lift

For every three children, gather
- Chair

introduce

What things can we do to show how strong we are? What are things we can't do? God made laws that tell how everything works. Today we'll explore laws that govern the way we move!

Do

1. Form trios and stand next to each other.

2. Center person extends arms. The other two grab his or her elbows and attempt to lift center person.

3. Next, center person presses elbows to sides. Other two grab elbows to lift.

4. Trade positions and try again so everyone has a turn. **Why does this work? What do you think makes the difference?**

5. Next, one person sits in a chair with back against the chair back. Another person presses a finger on sitter's forehead so that he or she cannot move forward. **Why can't the sitter rise?** Try it again so everyone has a turn.

why it works

These experiments illustrate a law about the body: Each of us has a center of gravity. The center of gravity is the place where most of our weight is concentrated. When our elbows are near our center of gravity, our friends lifted us more easily. When we couldn't move forward to shift our center of gravity over our legs, we couldn't lift ourselves out of the chair!

Prayer and Praise

Let's write a praise poem to God, using the letters of the word "gravity." Write the letters of the word down the side of a sheet of butcher paper, inviting students to add their ideas ("God, we praise You for gravity."). Read completed poem aloud as a prayer.

DAY SIX: Animals and People

Can You Hear Me Now?

For every two children, gather

- 20-foot (6-m) lengths of string (provide a variety: fishing line, twine, nylon string, etc.)

- 2 plastic cups, each with a hole punched in the center of its bottom

Introduce

How many of you have a telephone at home? A cell phone? Let's explore how our voices travel on a phone.

Do

1. Choose a string. Thread one end of it through the cup and tie a knot so that the long part hangs out of the bottom.

2. Thread the other end of the string through the second cup and knot string inside cup so that the string connects the cups as they face outward.

3. Stand as far from your partner as the string allows, stretching string taut. Talk into your cup while your partner holds cup to an ear. **How well can your partner hear you now?**

4. Trade assignments. **How softly can your partner talk and still be heard? Can you hear a whisper? What happens if you put your finger on the string?**

5. Now try using a different kind of string. **Does this string make a better or a worse cup phone? Why do you think so?**

large knot

Prayer and Praise

What part of you traveled over the string in this experiment? (Voice.) **God gave you a unique voice. It is not like anyone else's! Let's use our voices to thank Him.** Students choose to sing a song of praise together or take turns to pray aloud. (Optional: Students pray aloud into cup while partner listens.)

Why it works

Vibrations from your vocal cords travel through the string to your partner's cup. Your partner's cup collects the vibrations and makes them louder. If anything touches the string, the vibrations go into that, so the connection breaks. Just like some kinds of string work better than others, there are kinds of wire that work better than others to carry vibrations in a wired telephone. But a cell phone carries vibrations by radio waves. Your voice may even go to a satellite before it goes to another phone!

DAY SIX: Animals and People

Heartbeater

For every four children, gather

- Small amount of modeling clay
- 4 to 6 paper matches (out of matchbook)
- Clock or watch with second hand

introduce

How many times do you think your heart beats in a minute? Today we'll try a new way to count our heartbeats—by *seeing* them!

Do

1. Make a tiny ball of clay.

2. Insert the end of a match into this ball. Flatten the ball against a tabletop.

3. Lay your arm flat on a table, palm side up.

4. Place the clay ball on the thumb side of your wrist. Move it around until you see the match begin to wiggle or vibrate.

5. Watch the vibrations for one minute. **How many beats were there?**

6. Run in place for one minute and then check your heartbeat again. **How has your heart rate changed?**

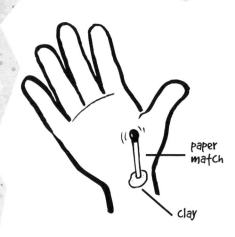

paper match

clay

why it works

There is a river of blood pumping through you! Your heart pumps blood through your blood vessels at a constant rate. The vessels in your wrist are close to the surface of your body, so it is easier to see the motion of your blood by counting the vibrations of the match.

Prayer and Praise

What happens to your heartbeat if you exercise? (Beats faster.) **God made our heart and blood system so that no matter what we are doing, our blood is moving enough oxygen to our cells!** Let's thank God for our hearts. Invite volunteers to place a hand over their heart as they pray, saying one word each time their heart beats!

DAY SIX: Animals and People

Fooling your Eye

For every child, gather
- Sheet of paper

introduce

When have you seen an optical illusion—something you saw that tricked your eye? Try this to fool your eye into thinking you have a hole in your hand!

Do

1. Roll the sheet of paper into a tube.

2. Hold the tube up to your right eye with your right hand.

3. Take a look. **What do you see?**

4. Now put your left hand in front of your face, touching the tube. Look with both eyes. **What do you see now? Why?**

5. Try sliding your left hand closer and farther along the tube. **What do you think makes the change in what you see?**

why it works

Each of your eyes sees from a slightly different angle. Your brain blends the images into one picture. When you look both through the tube and outside the tube, you send your brain two very different visual messages. Your brain combines them, so it looks like you have a hole in your hand! How did the image change when you moved your hand?

Prayer and Praise

What are some other things that fool our eyes? (Optical illusions. Mirages. Dots in printed pages. Pixels in video screens.) Our brains are pattern-seeking devices, always looking for an overall pattern. This helps our brains ignore some details that don't make sense. Our brains and eyes are wonderful gifts. Let's thank God for things we see, starting with the letter A. Students pray sentence prayers, naming items in alphabetical order. (Optional: Assign each student a section of the alphabet. Each student draws items he or she is thankful to see, in alphabetical order. Join sections into an alphabet prayer.)

DAY SIX: Animals and People

Penny trick

For every four children, gather

- 20 pennies

Introduce

What is something you touch every day? Something you don't like to touch? See if your sense of touch is able to help you do this trick smoothly.

Do

1. Line up five pennies.

2. Tell your partner to choose a penny while you close your eyes.

3. Tell partner to hold the penny tightly. Explain that you are going to be able to tell which penny he or she took even though your eyes are closed.

4. While your eyes are still closed, invite your partner to replace the penny in the line.

5. Open your eyes. Put your fingers close enough to feel the warmth from the pennies. Pick up the penny that is warmest.

6. Ask your partner if it is the correct penny. **How did your fingers help you?**

7. Switch roles and practice! (If penny is not warm enough, add time to step 3. Tell partner to count slowly backward from 10 with you.)

why it works

Touch is a gift from God. We sense not only pressure or pain but also heat or cold. Pennies are made of copper. Copper is a metal that conducts heat well. So when your partner held the penny, it heated up quickly. You could tell which one it was by heat! To do this at home, put the pennies in a cold place before trying the trick.

Prayer and Praise

Let's see if we can come up with 10 things our fingers can sense—one item for each finger. Students respond. Invite them to say sentence prayers, thanking God for the things our fingers can sense (heat, cold, etc.). (Optional: Students outline their hands on paper and write in each finger space something fingers can sense, adding a written prayer.)

DAY SIX: Animals and People

Heat Huddle

For every four children, gather

- 7 empty soda cans
- Hot water in a carafe
- Funnel
- 2 aquarium thermometers
- Clay or play dough
- Large rubber band

introduce

What animals have you seen sleeping together in a huddle? Why do you think they do this? How does huddling together in a group help animals stay warm?

Do

1. Pour hot water through funnel into each soda can.

2. Place one thermometer in each of two cans. Seal the tops around thermometers with clay or play dough.

3. Seal top holes of the other five cans with clay or dough.

4. Circle five cans around one can with a thermometer. Hold the 6 cans in a circle with the rubber band.

5. Set the seventh can by itself.

6. After 10 minutes, read the thermometers. **Which can is warmer? How big a difference is there in temperature? Why do you think this is so?**

why it works

The hot water molecules lose some of their energy through the can into the air. This made the cans cool. The can that stayed by itself cooled very quickly. But the can in the center of the others stayed very warm because the outer ones insulated the center one. Even though the cans on the outside of the circle lose more energy than the one on the inside, they still stayed warmer than the lone can. When penguins (and other animals) take turns to move to the outside of their huddle, they are using this principle of heat conservation.

Prayer and Praise

What are some other things we know about animals? Let's thank God for as many animals as we can, all the way through the alphabet! Students take turns to name an animal in a sentence prayer using alphabetical order. (Optional: Students draw and cut out animal shapes and then glue cutouts in a huddle on butcher paper, adding a written prayer.)

DAY SIX: Animals and People

Sight and Balance

For every four children, gather

- Stopwatch or a watch with a second hand
- Masking tape

introduce

What's the hardest athletic skill you've learned to do? Several senses often combine to help us do something. Here is a simple experiment to show how sight and balance work together.

Do

1. One person in the group becomes the timekeeper.

2. Other group members take this challenge: first, try standing on one foot for a whole minute.

3. Next, group members close their eyes and try to stand on one foot. Timekeeper checks watch to see who stood the longest on one foot.

4. Take turns so that the timekeeper gets to try the experiment, too. **What happened to your ability to stand on one foot when you closed your eyes?**

5. Now try walking a masking tape line while looking only at the end of the line. Then try walking it with your eyes closed. **What happens?**

why it works

These experiments prove that we need sight to help us balance—and to walk straight! When our eyes are closed, our brain doesn't have all the information it needs to help our body balance.

Prayer and Praise

The fact that our eyes actually help us balance is amazing. What are some other things about our bodies that are amazing? Let's thank God for some other amazing things about our bodies. Volunteers pray sentence prayers. (Optional: Students illustrate amazing facts about their bodies and add written prayers to papers.)

DAY SEVEN

Rest and Inertia

"By the seventh day God had finished the work he had been doing; so on the seventh day he rested from all his work. And God blessed the seventh day and made it holy, because on it he rested from all the work of creating that he had done."
Genesis 2:2-3

Here are experiments to tickle your interest in rest, inertia, kinetic energy and other laws of motion!

DAY SEVEN: Rest and Inertia

Walk and Rest

For every eight children, gather
- Yarn placed in a large circle on the floor
- Hand bell or whistle

Introduce

After God finished making the world, the Bible says He rested. Let's play a game where we try resting.

Do

1. Ring bell or blow whistle. Children walk single file around the outside of the yarn circle. Invite them to yawn and stretch as they walk.

2. Ring bell or blow whistle. Children quickly assume a resting position (lying, sitting with head on arms, etc.) outside of the yarn circle.

3. Ring bell or blow whistle again, calling out an action for children to do while moving around the circle (hop, march and clap, straddle yarn, etc.).

4. Play more rounds, inviting children to assume a different resting position each time they are at rest.

Why it Works

Everything that is alive has to rest. Every day, we need to rest, too. God gave us nighttime because He wants us to have time to rest.

Prayer and Praise

When it's time for bed, what do you do first? Second? Children respond. Let's pretend to get ready for bed. Children pantomime bedtime activities with you. Then pray a nighttime prayer, thanking God for rest. (Optional: Children draw pictures of nighttime activities and dictate nighttime prayers.)

DAY SEVEN: Rest and Inertia

ice Cube Slide

For every four children, gather

- Cookie sheet
- Blocks
- Ice cubes
- Fabric scraps (silk, corduroy, cotton, etc.)

introduce

When have you slid down a slide? Today we will experiment to see how ice cubes slide and how we can stop them from sliding so that they are at rest.

Do

1. Children use cookie sheets and blocks to build ramps.

2. Children take turns to slide ice cubes down the ramps. Invite children to adjust ramp angles by adding or removing blocks. **Do ice cubes move faster with a steeper ramp?**

3. Children lay a fabric piece on the ramp and try sliding ice cubes. **What happens?**

4. Children continue testing, using other types of fabric. **Which fabric makes the ice cubes stop and rest? Which fabric lets the ice cubes slide down?**

why it works

When we placed fabric on our slides, the fabric made the smooth cookie sheets less smooth. The roughness and rubbing is called friction. Friction slows down the ice cubes. Friction slows things down and also heats things up.

Prayer and Praise

Are your hands cold from the ice? Rub your hands together. That is friction, too! Friction can warm your cold hands. Let's thank God for His wise way of making our world. Let's repeat this poem: God is wise. He made our world. God made all things very good! Repeat together several times. (Optional: Children paint with ice cubes on paper sprinkled with dry tempera powder as you repeat poem.)

DAY SEVEN: Rest and Inertia

Push your Pulse

introduce

When is your heartbeat slower or faster, when you are resting or when you move? Let's find out!

Do

1. Children lie on the floor quietly for a minute or two.

2. While children are lying down, invite them to feel the fronts of their necks on one side to find a place where they can feel a heartbeat (pulse). **You can ask an adult for help.**

3. Adult counts each child's heartbeats for 15 seconds and then multiplies the number by 4 (resting heart rate). Adult writes child's name on paper and his or her resting heart rate.

4. Children march in place and swing their arms for about 2 minutes.

5. Children feel their own heartbeat again. **Is your heartbeat faster? Slower?**

6. Adult counts child's heartbeats again for 15 seconds and then multiplies the number by 4, writing that number next to the child's resting heart rate. **Which number is bigger?**

why it works

When you rest or sleep, your heart rate is slower than when you move. When your muscles work, your muscles need more oxygen. To get more oxygen to your muscles, your heart must beat faster.

Prayer and Praise

Why do you think we sleep at night? (Tired. Parents make us.) **God made our bodies so that they need rest. Rest helps our bodies grow, heal and stay healthy. Let's thank God for rest. When I say your name, you can say, "Thank You, God, for rest."** (Optional: Each child draws a picture of the place he or she rests at night and dictates a prayer for an adult to add to picture.)

DAY SEVEN: Rest and Inertia

String zinger

For every two children, gather

- Top halves of two 1-liter plastic soda bottles
- Tape (electrical tape or masking tape)
- Two 12-foot (3.6-m) lengths of string

introduce

What did God do on the seventh day? Today we're going to make a toy that shows how something that is at rest can be moved by a force outside it.

Do

1. Tape the soda bottle halves together with mouths at opposite ends. This is your zinger.

2. Drop the strings through the holes.

3. In pairs, each of you holds one set of strings coming from the mouth of the zinger.

4. Take turns to snap your strings apart. **What happens to the zinger? Why?**

why it works

When the zinger is in the center and the strings aren't moving, the zinger is at rest. The law of inertia says that the zinger won't move unless an outside force makes it move. When you snap the strings apart, you create that outside force! The force pushes the zinger in the opposite direction. When your partner snaps his or her strings, the zinger meets an opposite pushing motion. That stops it and then sends it back in the other direction.

Prayer and Praise

God made natural laws about the way His universe works! What are some of these laws? (Gravity. Inertia. Motion.) **Let's thank Him silently.** (Optional: Students write prayers of thanks on their zingers.)

DAY SEVEN: Rest and Inertia

Chain of Motion

For every four children, gather

- 5 to 10 checkers
- Optional—marbles, dominoes

Introduce

When an object is still, we say it is at rest. What has to happen for the object to move? But did you know that energy can move *through* something resting to move something else?

Do

1. Set three checkers in a row.

2. While holding the center checker still, snap a side checker into the center checker with some force. **What happens?**

3. Add more checkers to your line. **Is the reaction the same? Different? Why do you think so?**

4. Take turns so that everyone has the chance to move the checkers.

5. Optional: Try this with marbles or dominoes.

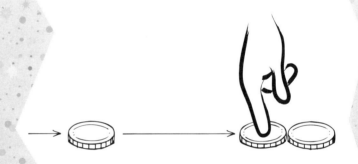

Why it works

The moving checker has energy (kinetic energy). That energy is transferred through the checker you held still. The energy moves into the end checker so that it scoots away!

Prayer and Praise

Let's form our own chain reaction with an add-on prayer. I'll start by thanking God for a creation that displays energy. The person next to me repeats what I said and then names another creation that displays energy, and so on. If anyone forgets, it's OK. We'll start over from there.

DAY SEVEN: Rest and Inertia

Kinetic Surprise

For every child, gather

- Plastic peanut butter jar with a center hole drilled in lid and in bottom

- 3 large metal nuts

- 6-inch (15-cm) length of string

- 3x⅛ inch (7.5x.3 cm) rubber band

- 2 toothpicks

- Optional—supplies for decorating jar (markers, glitter glue, etc.)

introduce

When something is at rest, it takes the energy from an outside force to make it move. Today we're going to store that energy inside these jars!

Do

1. Thread the string through the holes in the three metal nuts. Pull nuts together; knot string.

2. Tie and knot the string around the rubber band.

3. Place the nuts and rubber band inside the jar and then thread one end of rubber band through the lid. Slide a toothpick through the loop to hold it in place. Break off sharp ends of toothpick.

4. Ask a friend to help you pull out and hold the other end of the rubber band through the bottom of the jar while you secure with a toothpick as for the top.

5. Optional: Decorate jar if you'd like.

6. Screw on the lid, then roll the jar across the floor. **What happens? Why do you think it happens?**

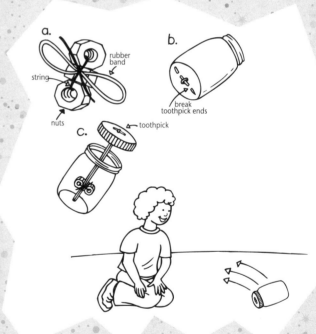

why it works

Why does the jar stop and then come back to you? It has stored kinetic energy inside. Kinetic energy is the energy of motion. As the jar rolls, the rubber band twists, which stores up that energy. When the jar stops, the rubber band unwinds. That releases the stored kinetic energy, so the jar rolls backward.

Prayer and Praise

Quick! In 30 seconds, let's name as many things as we can that display kinetic energy. (Car. Horse. Person. Spaceship.) After 30 seconds, invite students to thank God for a way they have seen kinetic energy displayed. (Optional: Students take turns to pantomime things that display kinetic energy while others guess.)

DAY SEVEN: Rest and Inertia

Friction-free Flying

For every four children, gather

- Scissors
- Variety of recyclable containers (cups, bowls, tops of plastic soda bottles, funnels, etc.)
- Hand-held hair dryer (blow-dryer)
- Optional: Carpet samples (if in an uncarpeted room)

introduce

Is it easier to walk through water or through air? Why? Moving through water makes more friction, the drag that slows things down and makes it harder to move. Let's experiment with a way to move that has no friction!

Do

1. Use scissors to make a hole in the center of any recyclable item you have.

2. Plug in the hair dryer and blow air (on the cool setting) through the hole. **How can you make the item move around the floor or table by moving the hair dryer? How do you think this works?**

3. Test other items. **Which shape of item moves best? Can you make the item move a little by simply blowing into the hole? Where have you seen a real hovercraft?**

why it works

What we have done is to make hovercraft. These little hovercraft travel on air produced by the hair dryers. A real hovercraft travels across water. It uses fans to blow air under the craft to create a cushion of air. Moving on a cushion of air produces far less friction than moving through water, so the hovercraft can go much faster than a boat of the same size.

Prayer and Praise

Friction can slow us down, but what if there were no friction? Would it be easy or hard to walk? What is another effect of friction? Invite students to rub their hands together and tell. Invite three volunteers to thank God for air, for inventions and for friction. (Optional: Students write prayers of thanks to God on hovercraft items.)

DAY SEVEN: Rest and Inertia

Boogie Bugs

For every four children, gather

- 4 hoops cut from a toilet paper tube, each ¾ inches (1.9 cm) across
- Card stock with 8 patterns traced (2 for each child, see below)
- Scissors
- Craft glue
- Construction paper
- 4 small marbles
- Tape
- Wiggle eyes

introduce

We're going to make toys today. These toy bugs don't crawl; they roll! Think about what laws of motion these toys demonstrate as we play with them.

Do

1. Slightly squeeze your toilet paper tube hoop into an oval.

2. Cut card stock for side pieces.

3. Glue one piece onto the edge of the hoop. Let it dry while you cut the legs, antennae, etc., from construction paper.

4. Place a marble inside the hoop and then glue the other side piece onto other edge. (If time is short, tape edges to reinforce the sides.)

5. Glue on legs, antennae, etc., and let the glue dry.

6. Set your finished bug at the top of a gentle slope. Watch the way it moves. **Why does it move that way?**

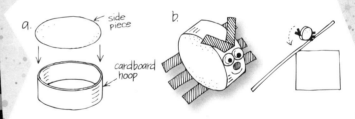

BUG PATTERN

why it works

According to the laws of motion, a marble should roll down a ramp at a constant speed. But because each marble is inside a hoop that is not round, it does not move at a constant speed. Instead, it lurches forward and takes the bug with it!

Prayer and Praise

God put many natural laws into motion to keep the universe functioning predictably. He also gave us creativity to think of new ways to use those laws. What are other ways people show the creativity God gave us? Students tell and then take turns to say sentence prayers, thanking God for a way people show creativity. (Optional: Volunteer takes a turn to say a sentence prayer while rolling his or her bug down a ramp.)

DAY SEVEN: Rest and Inertia

Lazy Painting

For every four children, gather

- Several colors of slightly thinned tempera paint in shallow cups
- 4 to 8 straws
- Paper

introduce

How do you think we can paint our papers? There aren't any brushes. Today we'll try the laziest, most restful way to get paint onto paper!

Do

1. Put a finger over the end of a straw.
2. Dip the open end of the straw into paint.
3. Lift straw out and over the place you want to place paint on your paper.
4. Lift your finger. **What happens? Does it work the same way every time?**
5. Try it without putting your finger over the end of the straw. **What happens? How is it different?**

why it works

Air is pressing on the surface of the paint. When you put the straw into the paint, the surface pressure pushes some paint up into the straw. But by putting a finger over the top of the straw, you keep air from pushing down through it. You equalize the pressure so that the paint stays in the straw. When you lift your finger, more air pushes down on the paint than is pushing up, so the paint comes out!

Prayer and Praise

God gave us brains and creative ability. That is one way we are created in His image. People have invented hundreds of ways to save their own energy or make life easier. Let's name some of them. (Car. Power lawnmower. Computer.) **Let's thank God for His gift of creative ability that makes it easier to rest!** Students pray sentence prayers, including the names of inventions, if desired. (Optional: Students draw pictures of inventions and write a prayer on paper.)

DAY SEVEN: Rest and Inertia

inertia Spinners

For every four children, gather

- 8 discarded CDs (or small paper plates with pencil-sized holes poked in centers)

- 8 pencils or dowels

- 48 pennies (12 for each child)

- Tape

introduce

The law of inertia means an object will keep doing what it's already doing. A rock will keep sitting until a force makes it move. A rolling marble will keep rolling until something stops it or it runs out of energy. Today we're going to see inertia at work when something spins.

Do

1. Count out six pennies. Tape them evenly onto the outer edge of a CD or plate.

2. Count out six more pennies. Tape them in a circle as closely around the center hole of another CD as you can.

3. Put a pencil through each CD. Tape it on both sides.

4. Predict: **Which of your CDs will spin faster? Why do you think so?**

5. Give one a spin. Then spin the other one. **Which wobbles more? Which spins better? Longer? What's your theory about the placement of pennies on spinning CDs?**

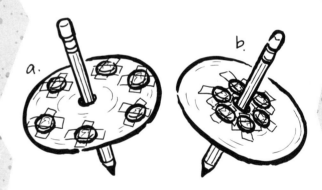

why it works

When more mass (weight of pennies) is placed at the outer edge of a spinning object, it increases the inertia. That means it will spin better. We increased its rotational inertia.

Prayer and Praise

What might happen if you added more pennies to the outer edge of the spinner that already has six pennies at its outer edge? Students tell. God gave us amazing brains. We can look at and think about the way He made our world. Let's thank Him for His love and kindness! Students respond to every phrase of your prayer with "Thank You for Your love and kindness." (Optional: Students draw and write prayers with markers on their spinners.)

BONUS RECIPES

Messy mixtures, amazing art materials and more!

Bathtub Finger Paint

Collect

½ cup pure soap flakes (Ivory Snow®)

¾ cup water

Food coloring

Mixer or wire whisk

Spray bottle filled with water

Do

Whip soap flakes with water until mixture is the consistency of shaving cream. Add a little food coloring. (Caution: Food coloring can stain grout.) Finger paint the sides of the tub, your legs, a mirror; spray with the bottle to remove paint.

cornstarch Paint

collect

3 teaspoons cornstarch

2 teaspoons white vinegar

Food coloring

Do

Mix cornstarch and vinegar. Add food coloring to achieve desired color.

190

corn Syrup Paint

collect

1 teaspoon corn syrup

1 tablespoon liquid tempera paint

Do

Mix corn syrup and tempera paint. When dry, paint will be shiny.

Cream-cheese Play Dough

Collect

8-ounce package of cream cheese, softened

½ cup nonfat dry milk

1 tablespoon honey

½ cup flour

Do

Combine cream cheese, milk and honey in a bowl and mix until well blended. Add approximately ½ cup flour to make dough workable. Children form shapes. (Optional: Place shapes on crackers for a snack.) Keep dough refrigerated. Discard dough on expiration date shown on cream cheese package.

Face Paint

Collect

3 tablespoons shortening

2 tablespoons cornstarch

Food coloring

Do

Mix shortening and cornstarch. Add food coloring to achieve desired color. Apply paint with fingers or small paintbrush with stiff bristles. Remove paint with soap and warm water.

Finger Paint

Collect

1 cup flour

1 cup water

1½ teaspoons salt

Food coloring

Do

Mix flour, water and salt. Add food coloring to achieve desired color.

Fruity watercolors

collect

Unsweetened Kool-Aid® packet(s)

2 teaspoons water (for each color)

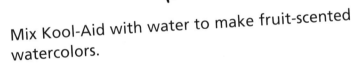

Do

Mix Kool-Aid with water to make fruit-scented watercolors.

Gak

Collect

Resealable plastic sandwich bag

3 tablespoons water

1 tablespoon white glue (not school glue)

2 heaping tablespoons borax (available at pharmacies or grocery stores)

Do

Put the water, glue and borax in bag. Seal bag and work ingredients with fingers to mix. Shape into a ball. If too sticky, roll in a little more borax.

Garden Mud

Collect

Large mixing bowl

Measuring cups

Large mixing spoons

2 cups sand

2 cups salt

2 cups dirt or potting soil (free of stones, etc.)

Water

Do

Children take turns to measure and mix together sand, salt and dirt or potting soil. Help children add enough water to make pliable dough. Allow time for children to explore the mud and make mud pies or sculptures of their choosing. Invite children to create their own garden scenes by adding materials (twigs, pebbles, etc.) to the mud dough.

Although this dough will not keep, children may experiment to see how long it takes mud dough shapes to dry in the sun.

Jiggly Dough

Collect

Large bowl

1 cup water

1 cup white glue

Food coloring

Large spoon

Powdered laundry detergent

Do

Put the water in the bowl. Invite children to take turns to add glue and food coloring and stir to make a thick mixture. Add powdered laundry detergent one tablespoon at a time until the liquid becomes a jiggly solid. Because the detergent is very absorbent, add only a little at a time. Playing with this dough will thicken it more. Store at room temperature in a sealed container. This dough is not edible and should not be left to dry on carpets or furniture.

Kool-Aid Paint

Collect

Unsweetened Kool-Aid packet(s)

¼ cup glue for each packet

Do

Mix one or more Kool-Aid packets into glue. Makes a thick, bright paint. Will also work as face paint. To thin paint, add water. Children paint with paintbrushes. When dry, the paint will be glossy.

Make your own Stickers

collect

2 tablespoons boiling water

1 tablespoon Jell-O®

Do

Mix boiling water with any flavor Jell-O. Paint cooled mixture onto backs of paper shapes or small pictures. Set shapes aside to dry. When dry, children may lick backs of Jell-O "stickers" and attach them to paper as desired.

Nectar Bubbles

Collect

1 cup water

1 tablespoon corn syrup

2 tablespoons dishwashing liquid

Large bowl

Do

Mix ingredients in a bowl and cover tightly. Works best if mixture sits for next-day use. Do not use in an area where bees or wasps will be present!

Potato Dough

Collect

Water

Large pot

Instant mashed potatoes

Milk

Salt

Butter

Mixing spoons

Small food items (chives, peas, carrot rounds, etc.)

Do

Prepare instant potatoes according to package directions. Add extra dry flakes as needed to stiffen mixture to a play dough consistency. (Children may help with this step.) Sculpt potato dough into shapes and use small food items to decorate. Then eat!

Puff Paint

Collect

⅓ cup glue

⅔ cup shaving cream

Optional—food coloring

Do

Mix glue with shaving cream. Mixture will puff up. (Optional: Add food coloring.) Children paint with craft sticks. (Note: Using equal parts of glue and shaving cream makes finger paint.)

Rock Salt Goo

Collect

1 cup white glue

1 cup rock salt

6 to 8 drops food coloring

Do

Mix rock salt and food coloring. Add glue and mix for several minutes. Children will enjoy using hands to play with the goo!

Salt and Flour Play Dough

collect

2 parts flour

1 part salt

1 tablespoon alum for every 2 cups flour

Food coloring

1 part water

Do

Mix dry ingredients well. Add food coloring to water to achieve desired color. Slowly pour colored water into dry ingredients; mix and add water until dough forms a ball around spoon. Knead dough on floured board. If dough is sticky, add more flour. If dough is too stiff, slowly add more water.

Salt, Flour and cornstarch Play Dough

Collect

1½ cups flour

1 cup cornstarch

1 cup salt

Food coloring

1¼ cups warm water

Do

Mix dry ingredients. Add food coloring to warm water. Slowly pour and mix colored water into dry ingredients until dough forms a ball around spoon. Knead dough on floured board. If dough is sticky, add more flour. If dough is too stiff, slowly add more water.

Sand Dough

Collect

1 cup sand

½ cup cornstarch

1 teaspoon granulated alum

¾ cup hot water

Pot

Spoon

Do

Mix dry ingredients in pot. Add hot water and stir vigorously. Cook over medium heat until thick, stirring constantly. Remove dough from pot and let cool. Knead dough for 20 to 30 seconds.

Sawdust Dough

Collect

2½ cups sawdust or commercially purchased wood shavings

1 cup flour

1 cup salt

1 cup water

Do

Mix dry ingredients well. Add water a little at a time, stirring until mixture reaches a stiff but pliable consistency. Add more flour and water if dough is too crumbly. Knead dough until it becomes elastic.

Shampoo Paint

Collect

3 teaspoons shampoo

Small amount of water

Food coloring

Do

Stir shampoo, water and food coloring until frothy.

Sidewalk Paint

Collect

¼ cup cornstarch

¼ cup water

Food coloring

Do

Mix cornstarch and water together. Stir in six to eight drops of food coloring. (Use additional food coloring for a more intense color.) Paint will wash off with water.

Soap Dough

Collect

2 cups soap flakes (Ivory® or Dreft®)

1 cup water

Mixing bowl and whisk

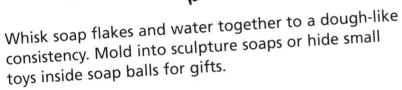

Do

Whisk soap flakes and water together to a dough-like consistency. Mold into sculpture soaps or hide small toys inside soap balls for gifts.

Super-Sandy Dough

Collect

4 cups sand

3 cups flour

Measuring cups

Mixing spoons

Large bowl

¼ cup vegetable oil

1 cup water

Optional—liquid dish detergent

Do

Invite volunteers to help you measure and mix sand and flour in a large bowl. Add oil to water (adjust as needed). Children take turns to mix wet ingredients into dry. Optional: Add a squirt or two of liquid dish detergent to soften dough. Give each child a fist-sized lump of dough to model as desired. To enrich this activity, provide small shells, seaweed, pieces of driftwood, etc., to add to dough.

Index

Activities Recommended for Mixed Age Groups

More Great Resources from Gospel Light

The Big Book of Bible Story Art Activities for Ages 3 to 6
Young children will love hearing favorite Bible stories as they enjoy creative art activities. Instructions for making puppets, collages, chalk art, friendship bracelets and more are provided to help children create Bible story art. Reproducible, perforated pages.
ISBN 08307.33086

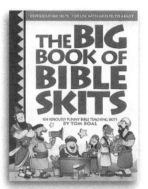

The Big Book of Bible Skits
Tom Boal

104 seriously funny Bible-teaching skits. Each skit comes with Bible background, performance tips, prop suggestions, discussion questions and more. Ages 10 to adult. Reproducible.
ISBN 08307.19164

The Really Big Book of Kids' Sermons and Object Talks with CD-ROM
This reproducible resource for children's pastors is packed with 156 sermons (one a week for three years) that are organized by topics such as friendship, prayer, salvation and more. Each sermon includes an object talk using a household object, discussion questions, prayer and optional information for older children. Reproducible.
ISBN 08307.36573

The Big Book of Volunteer Appreciation Ideas
Joyce Tepfer

This reproducible book is packed with 100 great thank-you ideas for teachers, volunteers and helpers in any children's ministry program. An invaluable resource for showing your gratitude!
ISBN 08307.33094

The Big Book of Christian Growth
Discipling made easy! 306 discussion cards based on Bible passages, and 75 games and activities for preteens. Reproducible.
ISBN 08307.25865

The Big Book of Bible Skills
Active games that teach a variety of Bible skills (book order, major divisions of the Bible, location references, key themes). Ages 8 to 12. Reproducible.
ISBN 08307.23463

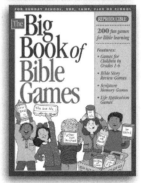

The Big Book of Bible Games
200 fun, active games to review Bible stories and verses and to apply Bible truths to everyday life. For ages 6 to 12. Reproducible.
ISBN 08307.18214

The Big Book of Bible Games #2
150 active games—balloon games, creative team relays, human bowling, and more—that combine physical activity with Bible learning. Games are arranged by Bible theme and include discussion questions. For grades 1 to 6. Reproducible.
ISBN 08307.30532

Gospel Light
God's Word for a Kid's World!™

To order, visit your local Christian bookstore or www.gospellight.com

How to Teach Children to Think and Act Like Jesus

"If people do not embrace Jesus Christ as their Savior before they reach their teenage years, the chance of their doing so at all is slim."

George Barna
Transforming Children into Spiritual Champions

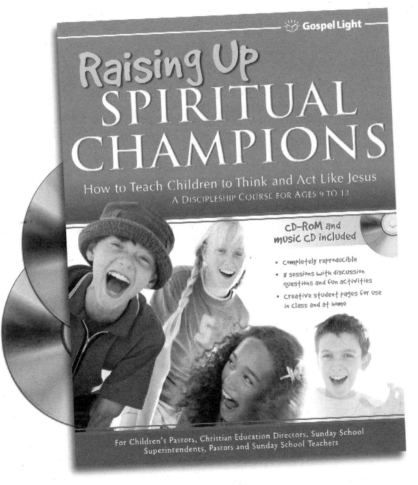

Raising Up Spiritual Champions
How to Teach Children to Think and Act Like Jesus
A Discipleship Course for Ages 9 to 12

Help kids answer the big questions about what it means to think and act like Jesus every day of their lives! This eight-session discipleship program provides the tools teachers need—from meaningful discussion questions to creative activities, from student pages to parent pages—to nurture lifelong spiritual growth in their students. Because most children's spiritual beliefs are in place by age 13, it's crucial that they acquire a biblical foundation for how they view themselves and the world. This program will help leaders teach God's truth during these all-important preteen years!

ISBN 08307.36638
Reproducible Manual
with CD-ROM and Music CD

Raising Up Spiritual Champions Includes

- CD-ROM containing everything in this book, including awards, **Student** and **Parent Pages**, publicity flyers, customizable forms, clip art and more!
- 8 reproducible sessions with discussion questions and fun activities
- Reproducible music CD with 12 praise and session-related songs
- How-tos for setting up the program
- 12 teacher-training articles
- **Student Pages** for use in class and at home to build discipleship habits
- **Parent Pages** that support parents in their role of spiritual teachers
- Teaching resources, including skits, discussion cards, games and more!

Available at your
Gospel Light supplier.

Gospel Light
God's Word for a Kid's World!™
www.gospellight.com